Be Faithful

It's always too soon to quit!

An expository study of the Pastoral Epistles, 1 and 2 Timothy and Titus

Warren W. Wiersbe

This book is designed for your personal reading pleasure and profit. It is also designed for group study. A Leader's Guide with helps and hints for teachers and visual aids (Victor Multiuse Transparency Masters) is available from your local bookstore or from the publisher.

VICTOR BOOKS

a division of SP

Offices also in Fullerton, California • Whitby, Ontario, Canada • Amersham-on-the-Hill, Bucks, England

Other books in Dr. Wiersbe's "Be" series:
Be Right (Romans)
Be Free (Galatians)
Be Rich (Ephesians)
Be Joyful (Philippians)
Be Complete (Colossians)
Be Ready (1, 2 Thessalonians)
Be Mature (James)
Be Real (1 John)

Books in Dr. Wiersbe's "Meet" series:
Meet Your King (Matthew, 26 chapters)
Meet Yourself in the Parables (13 of Jesus' parables)

Third printing, 1982

Cover photo by Martha Adair

Most of the Scripture quotations in this book are from the *King James Version* (KJV). Other quotations are from *The New International Version: New Testament* (NIV), © 1973 by The New York Bible Society; the *New American Standard Bible* (NASB), © 1960, 1962, 1963, 1968, 1971, 1973 by the Lockman Foundation, La Habra, California; *The New Testament in Modern English* (PH), © 1958, by J. B. Phillips, The Macmillan Company; and the *Amplified Bible* (AMP), © 1965 by Zondervan Publishing House.

Recommended Dewey Decimal Classification: 227.81
  Suggested Subject Headings: BIBLE, N.T.
  1 AND 2 TIMOTHY AND TITUS

Library of Congress Catalog Card Number: 81–50536
ISBN: 0–88207–268–4

VICTOR BOOKS
A Division of SP Publications, Inc.
P.O. Box 1825 • Wheaton, Illinois 60187

Contents

Dedicated with much love and appreciation
to some dear friends whose hearts
and homes have been opened to
me and my family:

ALLAN and JANE CARTER
Taunton, Somerset, England
HARVEY and ANN JOHNSON
West Bloomfield, Michigan
SPRAGUE and DOROTHY WILLARD
Chicago, Illinois

Preface

Timothy was not too happy in his church in Ephesus, and Titus was in a difficult situation on the Island of Crete. To both of them, Paul wrote: "Be faithful! It's always too soon to quit!"

Paul would want Christians in churches today to hear and heed this same message. Please don't get the idea that the Pastoral Epistles are only for pastors and other "full-time Christian workers." These three letters are for every Christian, every church member.

Paul used the Greek word *pistos* ("faithful") at least 17 times in these 3 letters. The theme runs through each chapter: Be faithful to the Word, be faithful to your task, be faithful to the people to whom you minister. God is faithful!

The late president of Wheaton College, Dr. V. Raymond Edman, used to remind Christians, "It's always too soon to quit." He was right, and those of us who dared to follow his counsel discovered that God gives staying power.

I want to accomplish two purposes in this book: (1) Help you understand the ministry of the local church, and (2) encourage you to *stick with it!* If you and I are faithful to the tasks God has given us, then His work will prosper and His name will be glorified. Could we ask for more?

Warren W. Wiersbe

Special note on the chronology of Paul's life

Paul was arrested in Jerusalem about the year A.D. 57, and kept in prison in Caesarea for two years (see Acts 21:19—26:32). Paul's voyage to Rome, to be tried before Caesar, started about September 59. After shipwreck and a three-month wait on Malta, he arrived in Rome, about February 60 (see Acts 27—28). There he lived in his own rented house and had liberty to minister.

Paul was acquitted of the charges against him and released. During the two years that followed, he ministered in various places and wrote 1 Timothy and Titus.

About the year 65 he was arrested again, and this time put into a dungeon. It was then that he wrote 2 Timothy, his last letter.

Ephesians, Philippians, and Colossians, as well as Philemon, were written during his first Roman captivity.

A suggested outline of 1 Timothy

Theme: how to manage the ministry of the local church (3:15)

I. THE CHURCH AND ITS MESSAGE—chapter 1
   1. Teaching sound doctrine (1:1-11)
   2. Proclaiming the Gospel (1:12-17)
   3. Defending the faith (1:18-20)

II. THE CHURCH AND ITS MEMBERS—chapters 2—3
   1. Praying men (2:1-8)
   2. Submitting women (2:9-15)
   3. Qualified pastors (3:1-7)
   4. Qualified deacons (3:8-13)
   5. Behaving believers (3:14-16)

III. THE CHURCH AND ITS MINISTER—chapter 4
   1. A good minister, preaching the Word (4:1-6)
   2. A godly minister, practicing the Word (4:7-12)
   3. A growing minister, progressing in the Word (4:13-16)

IV. THE CHURCH AND ITS MINISTRY—
chapters 5—6
1. To older members (5:1-2)
2. To older widows (5:3-10)
3. To younger widows (5:11-16)
4. To church officers (5:17-25)
5. To servants (slaves) (6:1-2)
6. To false teachers (6:3-10)
7. To the pastor (6:11-16, 20-21)
8. To the rich (6:17-19)

1
Stay on the Job!

1 Timothy 1

"Men wanted for hazardous journey, small wages, bitter cold, long months of complete darkness, constant danger, safe return doubtful. Honor and recognition in case of success."

That advertisement appeared in a London newspaper and *thousands of men responded!* It was signed by the noted Arctic explorer, Sir Ernest Shackleton, and that was what made the difference.

If Jesus Christ had advertised for workers, the announcement might have read something like this:

"Men and women wanted for difficult task of helping to build My church. You will often be misunderstood, even by those working with you. You will face constant attack from an invisible enemy. You may not see the results of your labor, and your full reward will not come till after all your work is completed. It may cost you your home, your ambitions, even your life."

In spite of the demands that He makes, Jesus Christ receives the "applications" of many who gladly give their all for Him. He is certainly the greatest Master for whom anyone could work, and the task of building His church is certainly the greatest challenge to which a believer could give his life.

Timothy was one young man who responded to Christ's call to help build His church. He was one of the Apostle Paul's special assistants. Along with Titus, Timothy tackled some of the tough assignments in the churches that Paul had founded. Timothy was brought up in a religious home (2 Tim. 1:5) and had been led to faith in Christ by Paul himself. This explains why Paul called Timothy "my own [genuine] son in the faith" (1 Tim. 1:2).

Timothy was born of mixed parentage: His mother was a Jewess, his father a Greek. He was so devoted to Christ that his local church leaders recommended him to Paul, and Paul added him to his "missionary staff" (Acts 16:1-5). Paul often reminded Timothy that he was chosen for this ministry (1 Tim. 1:18; 4:14). Timothy was faithful to the Lord (1 Cor. 4:17) and had a deep concern for God's people (Phil. 2:20-22).

But in spite of his calling, his close association with Paul, and his spiritual gifts, Timothy was easily discouraged. The last time Paul had been with Timothy, he had encouraged him to stay on at Ephesus and finish his work (1 Tim. 1:3). Apparently Timothy had physical problems (1 Tim. 5:23) as well as periods of discouragement, and you get the impression that some of the church members were not giving their pastor the proper respect as God's servant (1 Tim. 4:12; 2 Tim. 2:6-8).

Ephesus would not be the easiest place to pastor a church. (Are there any "easy places"? I doubt it.) The city was devoted to the worship of Diana, the patroness of the sexual instinct. Her lascivious images helped promote sexual immorality of all kinds (see Acts 19).

Paul had done a great work in Ephesus during his three-year ministry, so "all they which dwelt in [the province of] Asia heard the word of the Lord Jesus" (Acts 19:10). It was not easy for Timothy to follow a man like Paul! Of course, Satan had his workers in the city; for wherever there are spiritual opportunities there are also satanic obstacles (1 Cor. 16:8-9).

Paul wrote the letter we call 1 Timothy to encourage Timothy, to explain how a local church should be managed, and to enforce his own authority as a servant of God. In chapter 1 Paul explained the three responsibilities of a pastor and people in a local church.

1. Teach sound doctrine (1 Tim. 1:1-11)

From the very greeting of the letter, Paul affirmed his authority as a servant of Jesus Christ. Those who were giving Timothy trouble needed to remember that their pastor was there because God had put him there, for Paul's authority was given by God. Paul was an "apostle," one whom God sent with a special commission. His apostleship came by "commandment" from Jesus Christ. This word means "a royal commission." Both Paul and Timothy were sent by the King of kings!

Jesus Christ is not only Lord, but He is our "Saviour," a title used 10 times in the Pastoral Epistles (1 Tim. 1:1; 2:3; 4:10; 2 Tim. 1:10; Titus 1:3-4; 2:10, 13; 3:4, 6). To discouraged Timothy, the title "our hope" (1 Tim. 1:1) was a real boost. Paul wrote the same encouragement to Titus (1:2; 2:13; 3:7). Knowing that Jesus Christ is coming for us encourages us to serve Him faithfully.

One reason Christian workers must stay on the job is because false teachers are busy trying to capture Christians. There were teachers of false doctrines in Paul's day just as there are today, and we must take them seriously. These false teachers have no good news for lost sinners. They seek instead to lead Christians astray and capture them for their causes.

Paul used military language to help Timothy and his people see the seriousness of the problem (1 Tim. 1:3). "Charge" means "to give strict orders from a superior officer." Paul used this word (sometimes translated "Commandment" and "Command" in KJV) eight times in his two letters to Timothy (1 Tim. 1:3, 5, 18; 4:11; 5:7; 6:13, 17; 2 Tim. 4:1). He was conveying this idea: "Timothy, you are not only a pastor of the church in a difficult city. You are also a Christian soldier under orders from the King. Now pass these orders along to the soldiers in your church!"

What was the order? "Do not teach different doctrines from those taught by Paul!" In the original text there are 32 references to "doctrine," "teach," "teacher," "teaches," and "teaching" in the three Pastoral Epistles. In the early church, the believers were taught the Word of God and the meanings of basic Christian doctrines. In many churches today, the pulpit and choir loft are places for entertainment, not enlightenment and enrichment.

God had committed the truth of the Word to Paul (1 Tim. 1:11), and Paul had committed it to Timothy (6:20). It was Timothy's responsibility to guard the faith (2 Tim. 1:14) and to pass it along to faithful people (2:2).

Paul identified the false teaching as "fables and endless genealogies" (1 Tim. 1:4). Titus faced the same kind of false teaching in Crete (Titus 1:14; 3:9). The false teachers were using the Old Testament Law, and especially the genealogies, to manufacture all kinds of novelties; and these new doctrines were leading people astray. The false teachers were raising questions, not answering them. They were not promoting "God's saving plan" ("godly edifying," 1 Tim. 1:4), but were leading people away from the truth. Instead of producing love, purity, a good conscience, and sincere faith, these novel doctrines were causing division, hypocrisy, and all sorts of problems.

Paul used the word "conscience(s)" 21 times in his letters, and six of these references are in the Pastoral Epistles (1 Tim. 1:5, 19; 3:9; 4:2; 2 Tim. 1:3; Titus 1:15). The word "conscience" means "to know with." Conscience is the inner judge that accuses us when we have done wrong and approves when we have done right (Rom. 2:14-15). It is possible to sin against the conscience so that it becomes "defiled" (Titus 1:15). Repeated sinning hardens the conscience so that it becomes "seared" like scar tissue (1 Tim. 4:2).

It is tragic when professed Christians get off course because they refuse "healthy doctrine" ("sound doctrine," 1 Tim. 1:10). Paul also calls it "the doctrine . . . according to godliness" (6:3), "sound words" (2 Tim. 1:13), "sound doctrine" (4:3; Titus 1:9; 2:1), "faith" (1:13; 2:2), and "sound speech" (2:8). But many prefer the "vain jangling" (1 Tim. 1:6) of those who teach novelties rather than the pure Word of God that produces holiness in lives. It is unfortunate today that we not only have "vain jangling" ("meaningless talk," NIV) in teaching and preaching, but also in music. Far too many songs not only teach *no* doctrine, but many even teach *false* doctrines. A singer has no more right to sing a lie than a teacher has to teach a lie.

The reason for this false doctrine was a misuse of the Old Testament Law. These false teachers did not understand the content or the purpose of God's Law. They were leading believers out of the liberty of grace (Gal. 5:1ff) into the bondage of legalism, a tragedy that still occurs today. The flesh (our old nature) loves religious legalism, because rules and regulations enable a person to *appear* holy without really having to change his heart.

Paul listed 14 kinds of people who were condemned by the Law (1 Tim. 1:9-10). This is one of several such lists in the New Testament (see Mark 7:20-23; Rom. 1:18-32; Gal. 5:19-21). The lawful use of the old Law is to expose, restrain, and convict the lawless. The Law cannot save lost sinners (Gal. 2:21; 3:21-29); it can only reveal their need for a Saviour. When a sinner believes on Jesus Christ, he is freed from the curse of the Law (Gal. 3:10-14); and the righteous demands of the Law are met by the indwelling Holy Spirit as a believer yields to God (Rom. 8:1-4).

Paul (1 Tim. 1:9-10) centered particularly on five of the Ten Commandments in Exodus 20:

No. 5—*"Honor thy father and thy mother"*—
    "murderers of the fathers and . . . mothers."

No. 6—*"Thou shalt not kill [murder]"*—
    "murderers of fathers and . . .
    mothers . . . manslayers."

No. 7—*"Thou shalt not commit adultery"*—
    "whoremongers [fornicators] . . . them that de-
    file themselves with mankind [sodomites]."

No. 8—*"Thou shalt not steal"*—"men-stealers [kidnap-
    pers]."

No. 9—*"Thou shalt not bear false witness"*—
    "liars. . . . perjured persons."

It is the "glorious Gospel" that saves lost sinners. Paul had experienced the power of that Gospel (Rom. 1:16), and he had been entrusted with the ministry of the Gospel (1 Thes. 2:4). Law and Gospel go together, for the Law without the Gospel is diagnosis without remedy; but the Gospel without Law is only the Good News of salvation for people who don't believe they need it because they have never heard the bad news of judgment. The Law is not Gospel, but the Gospel is not lawless (Rom. 3:20-31).

2. Proclaim the Gospel (1 Tim. 1:12-17)

The mention of "the Gospel of the glory of the blessed God" (literal translation, 1:11) moved Paul to share his own personal testimony. He was "Exhibit A" to prove that the Gospel of the grace of God really works. When you read Paul's testimony (see also Acts 9:1-22; 22:1-21; 26:9-18), you begin to grasp the wonder of God's grace and His saving power.

A. WHAT PAUL USED TO BE (1 TIM. 1:13a). He was a *blasphemer* because he denied the deity of Jesus Christ and forced others to deny it. He was a *persecutor* who used physical power to try to destroy the church. "Murderous threats" were the very breath of his life (Acts 9:1, NIV). He persecuted the Christian church (1 Cor. 15:9) and then discovered that he was actually laying hands on Jesus Christ, the Messiah! (Acts 9:4) When Paul was Saul the rabbi, he consented to the stoning of Stephen and made havoc of the church (Acts 8:1-4).

Paul was *injurious*, a word that means "proud and insolent." A modern equivalent might be "bully." It conveys the idea of a haughty man "throwing his weight around" in violence. But the basic causes of his godless behavior were "ignorance" and "unbelief." Even though Saul of Tarsus was a brilliant man and well-educated (Acts 22:3; Gal. 1:13-14), his mind was blinded from the truth (2 Cor. 4:3-4; 1 Cor. 2:14). He was a religious man, yet he was not headed for heaven! It was not until he put faith in Jesus Christ that he was saved (Phil. 3:1-11).

B. HOW PAUL WAS SAVED (1 TIM. 1:13b-15). How could a holy God ever save and forgive such a self-righteous sinner? The key words are "mercy" and "grace." God in His mercy did not give Paul what he did deserve; instead God in His grace gave Paul what he did not deserve. Grace and mercy are God's love in action, God's love *paying a price* to save lost sinners. It is not God's love alone that saves us, for God loves the whole world (John 3:16). It is by grace that we are saved (Eph. 2:8-9) because God is rich in mercy (2:4) and grace (2:7).

What did Paul's "ignorance" have to do with his salvation? Is ignorance an excuse before God? Of course not! The fact of his ignorance is related to a special Jewish law (Lev. 5:15-19; Num. 15:22-31). If a person sinned knowingly "with a high hand" in Israel, he was cut off from the people. But if he sinned in ignorance, he was permitted to bring the proper sacrifices to atone for his sins. Jesus recognized this principle when He prayed on the cross, "Father, forgive them, for they know not what they do" (Luke 23:34). Their ignorance did not save them, nor did Christ's prayer save them; but the combination of the two postponed God's judgment, giving them an opportunity to be saved.

Paul stated that it took "exceedingly abundant" grace to save him! Paul liked to use the Greek prefix *huper* (meaning "an exceeding abundant amount"), and he often attached it to words in his letters. You might translate some of these as "super-increase of faith" (2 Thes. 1:3); "super-abounding power" (Eph. 1:19); "super-conqueror" (Rom. 8:37). This same prefix has come into the English language as *hyper*. We speak of "hyperactive" children and "hypersensitive" people.

Paul makes it clear that this salvation is not for him only, but for all who receive Jesus Christ (1 Tim. 1:15). If Jesus could save Saul of Tarsus, the *chief* of sinners, then He can save anybody! We admire Paul's humility, and we note that he considered himself to be the "least of the apostles" (1 Cor. 15:9) and the "least of all saints" (Eph. 3:8). Notice that Paul did not write "of whom I *was* chief," but "of whom I *am* chief."

C. WHAT PAUL BECAME (1 TIM. 1:12, 16). The grace of God turned the persecutor into a preacher, and the murderer into a minister and a missionary! So dramatic was the change in Paul's life that the Jerusalem church suspected that it was a trick, and they had a hard time accepting him (Acts 9:26-31). God gave Paul his ministry; he did not get it from Peter or the other apostles (Gal. 1:11-24). He was called and commissioned by the risen Christ in heaven.

God saw that Paul was faithful, and so He entrusted the Gospel to him. Even as an unbelieving and Gospel-ignorant rabbi, Paul had maintained a good conscience as he lived up to the light that he had. So often those who are intensely wrong as lost sinners become intensely right as Christians and are greatly used of God to win souls. God not only *entrusted* the Gospel to Paul, but He *enabled* Paul to minister that Gospel (Phil. 4:13; 1 Cor. 15:10). When someone obeys God's call to serve, God always equips and enables that person.

But Paul not only became a minister; he also became *an example* (1 Tim. 1:16). In what sense is Paul an example to lost sinners who believe on Christ? None of us has had the same experience that Paul had on the Damascus road (Acts 9). We did not see a light, fall to the ground, and hear Jesus speak from heaven. But Paul is a pattern ("type") to all lost sinners, for he was the chief of sinners! He is proof that the grace of God can change *any* sinner!

But there is a special application of this to today's people of Israel, Paul's countrymen, for whom he had a special burden (Rom. 9:1-5; 10:1-3). The people of Israel, like unconverted Saul of Tarsus, are religious, self-righteous, blind to their own Law and its message of the Messiah, and unwilling to believe. One day, Israel shall see Jesus Christ even as Paul saw Him; and the nation shall be saved. "They shall look upon Me whom they have pierced" (Zech. 12:10). This may be one reason why Paul said he was "born out of due time" (1 Cor. 15:8), for his experience of seeing the risen Christ came at the beginning of this church age and not at its end (Matt. 24:29ff).

3. Defend the faith (1 Tim. 1:18-20)

Paul gave a third responsibility for the local church to fulfill, besides teaching sound doctrine and proclaiming the Gospel.

Again, Paul used military language to enforce his statement, for the word "change" (1:18) means "an urgent command handed down from a superior officer" (1:3). Paul also reminded Timothy that God had chosen him for his ministry. Apparently some of the prophets in the local assemblies had been led by the Spirit to select Timothy for service (see Acts 13:1-3 for an example of this procedure).

It was not easy to serve God in pagan Ephesus, but Timothy was a man under orders, and he had to obey. The soldier's task is to "please him who hath chosen him to be a soldier" (2 Tim. 2:4), and not to please himself. Furthermore, Timothy was there by divine appointment: God had chosen him and sent him. It was this fact that could give him assurance in difficult days. If you are God's servant, called by the Spirit, obeying His will, then you can "stay with it" and finish the work. These assurances enabled Timothy to war the good warfare.

Paul changed the illustration from army to navy (1 Tim. 1:19). He warned Timothy that the only way to succeed was to hold fast to "faith and a good conscience." It is not enough to proclaim the faith with our lips; we must practice the faith in our daily lives. One man said of his hypocritical pastor, "He is such a good preacher, he should never get out of the pulpit; but he is such a poor Christian, he should never get into the pulpit!"

A good conscience is important to a good warfare and a good ministry. H. L. Mencken defined conscience as "the inner voice which warns us that somebody may be looking." But a man with a good conscience will do the will of God in spite of who is watching or what people may say. Like Martin Luther, he will say, "Here I stand, I can do no other, so help me God!"

Professed Christians who "make shipwreck" of their faith do so by sinning against their consciences. Bad doctrine usually starts with bad conduct, and usually with secret sin. Hymenaeus and Alexander deliberately rejected their good consciences in order to defend their ungodly lives. Paul did not tell us exactly what they did, except that their sin involved "blaspheming" in some way. Hymenaeus said that the resurrection was already past (2 Tim. 2:16-18). Alexander was a popular name in that day, so we cannot be sure that the man named in Paul's next letter to Timothy (2 Tim. 4:14) is the same man; but if he is, no doubt he withstood Paul by teaching false doctrine.

"Delivered unto Satan" (1 Tim. 1:20) implies apostolic discipline (see 1 Cor. 5:5) and disassociation from the local church. The verb "learn" (1 Tim. 1:20) means "to learn by discipline." When a Christian refuses to repent, the local fellowship should exercise discipline, excluding him from the protective fellowship of the saints, making him vulnerable to the attacks of Satan. The fellowship of the local church, in obedience to the will of God, gives a believer spiritual protection. Satan has to ask God for permission to attack a believer (see Job 1—2 and Luke 22:31-34).

Each local church is in a constant battle against the forces of evil. There are false prophets and false teachers, as well as false christs. Satan is the originator of false doctrines, for he is a liar from the beginning (John 8:44). It is not enough for a local church to teach sound doctrine and to proclaim the Gospel. The church must also defend the faith by exposing lies and opposing the doctrines of demons (1 Tim. 4:1).

It is important that our ministry be balanced. Some churches only preach the Gospel and seldom teach their converts the truths of the Christian life. Other churches are only opposing false doctrine; they have no positive ministry. We must be teachers of healthy doctrine ("sound doctrine," 1 Tim. 1:10) or the believers will not grow. We must preach the Gospel and keep winning the lost to Christ. And we must defend the faith against those who would corrupt the church with false doctrine and godless living. It is a constant battle, but it must be carried on.

Timothy must have been greatly helped and encouraged when he read this first section of Paul's letter. God had called Timothy, equipped him, and put him into his place of ministry. Timothy's job was not to run all over Ephesus, being involved in a multitude of tasks. His job was to care for the church by winning the lost, teaching the saved, and defending the faith. Any task that did not relate to these ministries would have to be abandoned. One reason some local churches are having problems is that the pastors and spiritual leaders are involved in too many extracurricular activities and are not doing the tasks God has called them to do.

It might be a good idea for our churches to take a spiritual inventory!

2
Service—or Circus?

1 Timothy 2

"Let all things be done decently and in order" (1 Cor. 14:40) is a basic principle for the conduct of the ministry of the church. Apparently young Timothy was having some problems applying this principle to the assemblies in Ephesus. The public worship services were losing their order and effectiveness because both the men and the women members of the church were disobeying God's Word.

"The church is an organism," a pastor told me, "so we shouldn't put too much emphasis on organization. We should allow the Spirit to have freedom."

"But if an organism is *disorganized*," I replied, "it will die. Yes, we must permit the Spirit to have freedom, but even the Holy Spirit is not free to disobey the Word of God."

Often, what we think is the "freedom of the Spirit" are the carnal ideas of some Christian who is not walking in the Spirit. Eventually this "freedom" becomes anarchy, and the Spirit grieves as a church gradually moves away from the standards of God's Word.

To counteract this tendency, Paul exhorted both the men and the women in the church and reminded them of their spiritual responsibilities.

1. The men—praying (1 Tim. 2:1-8)

A. THE PRIORITY OF PRAYER (1 TIM. 2:1A). "First of all" indicates that prayer is most important in the public worship of the church. It is sad to see how prayer has lost importance in many churches. "If I announce a banquet," a pastor said, "people will come out of the woodwork to attend. But if I announce a prayer meeting, I'm lucky if the ushers show up!" Not only have the special meetings for prayer lost stature in most local churches, but even prayer *in the public services* is greatly minimized. Many pastors spend more time on the announcements than they do in prayer!

My good friend Peter Deyneka, Sr., founder of the Slavic Gospel Association, has often reminded me: "Much prayer, much power! No prayer, no power!" Prayer was as much a part of the apostolic ministry as preaching the Word (Acts 6:4). Yet some pastors spend hours preparing their sermons, but never prepare their public prayers. Consequently, their prayers are routine, humdrum, and repetitious. I am not suggesting that a pastor write out every word and read it, but that he think through what he will pray about. This will keep "the pastoral prayer" from becoming dull and a mere repetition of what was "prayed" the previous week.

But the church members also need to be prepared to pray. Our hearts must be right with God and with each other. We must really want to pray, and not pray simply to please people (as did the Pharisees, Matt. 6:5), or to fulfill a religious duty. When a local church ceases to depend on prayer, God ceases to bless its ministry.

B. THE VARIETY OF PRAYER (1 TIM. 2:1B). There are at least seven different Greek nouns for "prayer," and four of them are used here. *Supplications* carries the idea of "offering a request for a felt need."

Prayers is the commonest term for this activity, and it emphasizes the sacredness of prayer. We are praying *to God*; prayer is an act of worship, not just an expression of our wants and needs. There should be reverence in our hearts as we pray to God.

Intercessions is best translated *petitions*. This same word is translated "prayer" in 1 Timothy 4:5, where it refers to blessing the food we eat. (It is rather obvious that we do not *intercede* for our food in the usual sense of that word.) The basic meaning of the word is "to draw near to a person and converse confidently with him." It suggests that we enjoy fellowship with God so that we have confidence in Him as we pray.

Giving of thanks is definitely a part of worship and prayer. We not only give thanks for answers to prayer, but for who God is and what He does for us in His grace. We should not simply add our thanksgiving to the end of a selfish prayer! Thanksgiving should be an important ingredient throughout all of our prayers. In fact, sometimes we need to imitate David and present to God *only* thanksgiving with no petitions at all! (See Ps. 103.)

"Prayer and supplication [petition] with thanksgiving" are a part of Paul's formula for God's peace in our hearts (Phil. 4:6). It is worth noting that Daniel, the great prayer warrior, practiced this kind of praying (Dan. 6:10-11).

C. THE OBJECTS OF PRAYER (1 TIM. 2:1C-2). "All men" make it clear that no person on earth is outside the influence of believing prayer. (We have no examples of exhortations that say we should pray for the dead. If we were, Paul certainly had a good opportunity to tell us in this section of his letter.) This means we should pray for the saved and the lost, for people near us and people far away, for enemies as well as friends. Unfortunately, the Pharisees did not have this universal outlook in their prayers, for they centered their attention primarily on Israel.

Paul urged the church to especially pray for those in authority. Godless Emperor Nero was on the throne at that time, and yet the believers were supposed to pray for him! Even when we cannot respect men or women in authority, we must respect their offices and pray for them. In fact, it is for our own good that we do so: "that we may live peaceful and quiet lives in all godliness and holiness" (2:2b, NIV). The early church was always subject to opposition and persecution, so it was wise to pray for those in authority. "Quiet" refers to circumstances around us, while "peaceable" refers to a calm attitude within us. The results should be lives that are godly and honorable.

To be sure, Paul has not named all the persons we can and should pray for, since "all men" cover the matter fully. We can't pray for everybody in the world by name, but we certainly ought to pray for those we know and know about. Why? Because it is a good thing to do, and because it pleases God.

D. THE REASONS FOR PRAYER (1 TIM. 2:3-4). The word "good" is a key word in Paul's pastoral epistles (1:8, 18; 2:3; 3:1, 7, 13; 4:4, 6; 5:4, 10, 25; 6:12-13, 18-19; 2 Tim. 1:14; 2:3; 4:7; Titus 2:7, 14; 3:8, 14). The Greek word emphasizes the idea of something being intrinsically good, not just good in its effects. "Fair" and "beautiful" are synonyms. Certainly prayer of itself is a goodly practice, and brings with it many good benefits.

But prayer is also pleasing to the Lord. It pleases the Father when His children pray as He has commanded. The Pharisees prayed to be praised by men (Matt. 6:5) or to impress other worshipers (Luke 18:9-14). True Christians pray in order to please God. This suggests that we must pray in the will of God, because it certainly does not please the Father when we pray selfishly (James 4:1-10; 1 John 5:14-15). It's often said that the purpose of prayer is not to get man's will done in heaven, but to get God's will done on earth.

What is God's will? The salvation of lost souls, for one thing. We can pray for "all men" because it is God's will that "all men" come to the knowledge of salvation through faith in Jesus Christ. God loved the world (John 3:16) and Christ died for the whole world (1 John 2:2; 4:14). Jesus died on the cross that He might draw "all men" to salvation (John 12:32). This does not mean all people without *exception*, for certainly the whole world is not going to be saved. It means all people without *distinction*—Jews and Gentiles, rich and poor, religious and pagan.

If God doesn't want anyone to perish, then why are so many lost? God is long-suffering with lost sinners, even delaying His judgment that they might come to Christ (2 Peter 3:9). But salvation depends on a "knowledge of the truth" (1 Tim. 2:4). Not everyone has heard the truth of the Gospel, and many who have heard have rejected it. We cannot explain the mystery of God's sovereignty and man's responsibility (see John 6:37), but realize that both are taught in the Bible and are harmonized in God's great plan of salvation. We do know that prayer is an important part of God's program for reaching a lost world. We have the responsibility of praying for lost souls (Rom. 10:1) and making ourselves available to share the Gospel with others.

E. THE BASIS FOR PRAYER (1 TIM. 2:5-7). Many believers do not realize that prayer is based on the work of Jesus Christ as Saviour and Mediator. As the God-Man, Jesus Christ is the perfect Mediator between a holy God and His failing children. One of Job's complaints had to do with the absence of a mediator who could take his message to the throne of God. "There is no umpire between us, who may lay his hand upon us both" (Job 9:33, NASB).

Since there is only one God, there is need for only one Mediator; and that Mediator is Jesus Christ. *No other person can qualify*. Jesus Christ is both God and man, and therefore can be the "umpire" between God and man. In His perfect life and substitutionary death, He met the just demands of God's holy law. He was the "ransom for all." The word "ransom" means "a price paid to free a slave." His death was "on behalf of all." Though the death of Christ is efficient only for those who trust Him, it is sufficient for the sins of the whole world. Jesus said that He came "to give His life a ransom for many" (Matt. 20:28).

Christ died for "all men," and God is willing for "all men to be saved." How does this Good News get out to a sinful world? God calls and ordains messengers who take the Gospel to lost sinners. Paul was such a messenger: he was a *preacher* (the herald of the king), an *apostle* (one sent with a special commission), and a *teacher*. The same God who ordains *the end* (the salvation of the lost) also ordains *the means to the end:* prayer and preaching of the Word. This Good News is not for the Jews only, but also for the Gentiles.

If the basis for prayer is the sacrificial work of Jesus Christ on the cross, then prayer is a most important

activity in a church. Not to pray is to slight the Cross!
To pray only for ourselves is to deny the worldwide
outreach of the Cross. To ignore lost souls is to ignore
the Cross. "All men" [people] is the key to this paragraph: We pray for "all" because Christ died for "all"
and it is God's will that "all" be saved. We must give
ourselves to God to be a part of His worldwide program to reach people before it is too late.

F. THE ATTITUDE IN PRAYER (1 TIM. 2:8). Paul stated
definitely that "men" should pray in the local assembly. Both men and women prayed in the early church
(1 Cor. 11:4-5), but the emphasis here is on the men. It
is common to find women's prayer meetings, but not
often do we find men's prayer meetings. If the men do
not pray, the local church will not have dedicated
leaders to oversee its ministry.

It was customary for Jewish men to pray with their
arms extended and their hands open to heaven. Our
traditional posture of "bowing the head, folding the
hands, and closing the eyes" is nowhere found or
commanded in Scripture. Actually, there are many
prayer postures found in the Bible: standing with out-
stretched hands (1 Kings 8:22); kneeling (Dan. 6:10);
standing (Luke 18:11); sitting (2 Sam. 7:18); bowing the
head (Gen. 24:26); lifting the eyes (John 17:1); falling
on the ground (Gen. 17:3). The important thing is not
the posture of the body but the posture of the heart.

Paul stated three essentials for effective prayer, and
the first was "holy hands." Obviously this means a holy
life, a clean heart. "Clean hands" were symbolic of a
blameless life (Ps. 24:4; 2 Sam. 22:21). If we have sin in
our lives, we cannot pray and expect God to answer
(Ps. 66:18).

"Without wrath" is the second essential, and it requires that we be on good terms with one another.

"Without anger" might be a better translation. A person who is constantly having trouble with other believers, who is a troublemaker rather than a peacemaker, cannot pray and get answers from God.

"Doubting" suggests that we must pray *in faith*, but the word really means "disputing." When we have anger in the heart, we often have open disagreements with others. Christians should learn to disagree without being disagreeable. We should "do all things without murmurings and disputings" (Phil. 2:14).

Effective praying, then, demands that I be in a right relationship with God ("holy hands") and with my fellow believers ("without murmurings and disputings"). Jesus taught the same truth (Mark 11:24-26). If we spent more time *preparing* to pray and getting our hearts right before God, our prayers would be more effective.

2. The women—submitting
(1 Tim. 2:9-15)

In these days of "Women's Lib" and other feminist movements, the word "submission" makes some people see red. Some well-meaning writers have even accused Paul of being a "crusty old bachelor" who was anti-women. Those of us who hold to the inspiration and authority of the Word of God know that Paul's teachings came from God and not from himself. If we have a problem with what the Bible says about women in the church, the issue is not with Paul (or Peter—see 1 Peter 3:1-7), but with the Lord who gave the Word (2 Tim. 3:16-17).

The word translated "subjection" in 1 Timothy 2:11 is translated "submitting" and "submit" in Ephesians 5:21-22 and Colossians 3:18. It literally means "to rank under." Anyone who has served in the armed forces knows that "rank" has to do with order and authority, and not with value or ability. A colonel is higher in rank than a private, but that does not necessarily mean that the colonel is a better man than the private. It only means that the colonel has a higher rank and therefore more authority.

"Let all things be done decently and in order" (1 Cor. 14:40) is a principle God follows in His Creation. Just as an army would be in confusion if there were no levels of authority, so society would be in chaos without submission. Children should submit to their parents because God has given parents the authority to train their children and discipline them in love. Employees should submit to employers and obey them (Eph. 6:5-8, where the immediate reference is to household slaves, but the application can be made to workers today). Citizens should submit to government authorities, even if the authorities are not Christians (Rom. 13; 1 Peter 2:13-20).

Submission is not subjugation. Submission is recognizing God's order in the home and the church, and joyfully obeying it. When a Christian wife joyfully submits to the Lord and to her own husband, it should bring out the best in her. (For this to happen, the husband must love his wife and use God's order as a tool to build with, not a weapon to fight with—Eph. 5:18-33.) Submission is the key to spiritual growth and ministry: Husbands should be submitted to the Lord, Christians should submit to each other (5:21), and wives should be submitted to the Lord and to their husbands.

The emphasis in this section (1 Tim. 2:9-15) is on the place of women in the local church. Paul admonished these believing women to give evidence of their submission in several ways.

A. MODEST DRESS (1 TIM. 2:9). The contrast here is between the artificial glamour of the world and the true beauty of a godly life. Paul did not forbid the use of jewelry or lovely clothes, but rather the excessive use of them as substitutes for the true beauty of "a meek and quiet spirit" (see 1 Peter 3:1-6). A woman who depends only on externals will soon run out of ammunition! She may attract attention, but she will not win lasting affection. Perhaps the latest fashion fads were tempting the women in the church at Ephesus, and Paul had to remind Timothy to warn the women not to get trapped.

The word translated "modest" (1 Tim. 2:9) simply means "decent and orderly." It is related to the Greek word from which we get the English word "cosmetic." A woman's clothing should be decent, orderly, and in good taste. "Shamefacedness" literally means "modesty, the avoiding of extremes." A woman who possesses this quality is ashamed to go beyond the bounds of what is decent and proper. "Sobriety" comes from a Greek word that means "having a sound mind and good sense." It describes an inner self-control—a spiritual "radar"—that tells a person what is good and proper.

Ephesus was a wealthy commercial city, and some women there competed against each other for attention and popularity. In that day expensive hairdos arrayed with costly jewelry, were an accepted way to get to the top socially. Paul admonished the Christian women to major on the "inner person," the true beauty that only Christ can give. He did not forbid the use of nice clothing or ornaments. He cautioned balance and propriety, with the emphasis on modesty and holy character.

"It's getting harder and harder for a Christian

woman to find the right kind of clothes!" a church member complained to me one summer. "I refuse to wear the kind of swimsuits they're selling! Whatever happened to old-fashioned modesty?"

B. GODLY WORKS (1 TIM. 2:10). Paul did not suggest that good works are a substitute for clothing! Rather, he was contrasting the "cheapness" of expensive clothes and jewelry with the true values of godly character and Christian service. "Godliness" is another key word in Paul's pastoral letters (2:2, 10; 3:16; 4:7-8; 6:3, 5-6, 11; 2 Tim. 3:5; Titus 1:1). Glamour can be partially applied on the outside, but godliness must come from within.

We must never underestimate the important place that godly women played in the ministry of the church. The Gospel message had a tremendous impact on them, because it affirmed their value before God and their equality in the body of Christ (Gal. 3:28). Women had a low place in the Roman world, but the Gospel changed that.

There were devoted women who ministered to Jesus in the days of His earthly ministry (Luke 8:1-3). They were present at His crucifixion and burial, and it was a woman who first heralded the glorious news of His resurrection. In the Book of Acts we meet Dorcas (Acts 9:36ff), Lydia (16:14ff), Priscilla (18:1-3), and godly women in the Berean and Thessalonian churches (17:4, 12). Paul greeted at least eight women in Romans 16; and Phoebe, who carried the Roman epistle to its destination, was a deaconess in a local church (Rom. 16:1). Many believing women won their husbands to the Lord and then opened their homes for Christian ministry.

C. QUIET LEARNING (1 TIM. 2:11). "Silence" is an unfortunate translation, because it gives the impression that believing women were never to open their mouths in the assembly. This is the same word that is translated "peaceable" in verse 2. Some of the women abused their newfound freedom in Christ, and created disturbances in the services by interrupting. It is this problem that Paul addressed in this admonition. It appears that women were in danger of upsetting the church by trying to "enjoy" their freedom. Paul wrote a similar admonition to the church in Corinth (1 Cor. 14:34), though this admonition may apply primarily to speaking in tongues.

D. RESPECTING AUTHORITY (1 TIM. 2:12-15). Women *are* permitted to teach. Older women should teach the younger women (Titus 2:3-4). Timothy was taught at home by his mother and grandmother (2 Tim. 1:5; 3:15). But in their teaching ministry, they must not "lord it over" men. There is nothing wrong with a godly woman instructing a man in private (Acts 18:24-28); but she must not assume authority in the church and try to take the place of a man. She should exercise "quietness" and help keep order in the church.

Paul gave several arguments to back up this admonition that the Christian men in the church should be the spiritual leaders. The first is an argument from *Creation*: Adam was formed first, and then Eve (1 Tim. 2:12-13). (Paul used this same argument in 1 Cor. 11:1-10.) We must keep in mind that *priority* does not mean *superiority*. Man and woman were both created by God and in God's image. The issue is only authority: Man was created first.

The second argument has to do with man's fall into sin. Satan deceived the woman into sinning (2 Cor. 11:3; Gen. 3:1ff); the man sinned with his eyes wide open. Because Adam rejected the God-given order, he listened to his wife, disobeyed God, and brought sin and death into the world. The submission of wives to their own husbands is a part of the original Creation. The disorder we have in society today results from a violation of that God-given order.

I do not think Paul suggested that women are more gullible than men and thus more easily deceived; for experience proves that both men and women are deceived by Satan. On one occasion, Abraham listened to his wife and got into trouble (Gen. 16). Later on, she gave him counsel and God told him to obey it (Gen. 21). In my own pastoral ministry, I have benefited greatly from the encouragement and counsel of godly women; but I have tried not to let them usurp authority in the church. In fact, the godly women I have known have no desire to "run" things in the church.

The Creation of humans and their fall both seem to put the woman in an inferior position, but she does have a ministry from God (1 Tim. 2:15). There was probably a close relationship in Paul's mind between what he wrote here and what Moses wrote in Genesis 3:16—the promise of the Saviour who would be "made of a woman" (Gal. 4:4). It was through a woman that the Saviour came into the world. (Keep in mind that Jesus had an earthly mother but not an earthly father— Luke 1:34-35; Matt. 1:18ff.)

But Paul teaches a practical lesson (1 Tim. 2:15). He promised that the woman would "be kept safe through childbirth" (NIV) if "they" (both husband and wife) continued in sincere dedication to the Lord.

Does this mean that Christian mothers will never die in childbirth? History and experience both tell us that they do. God has His purposes, and His ways are far above our thoughts (Isa. 55:8-9). Paul laid down a general principle that encouraged the believing women of that day. Their ministry was not to "run" the church, but to care for the home and bear children to the glory of God (1 Tim. 5:14). Their home congregation would give them abundant opportunities for teaching the Word and ministering to the saints (see Rom. 16:1-6).

Godly women do have an important ministry in the local assembly, even though they are not called to be teachers of the Word in a pastoral sense. If all is done "decently and in order," then God will bless.

3
Follow the Leaders

1 Timothy 3

Everything rises or falls with leadership, whether it be a family or a local church. The Holy Spirit imparts gifts to believers for ministry in the local church, and among those gifts are "pastors and teachers" (Eph. 4:11) and "helps" and "governments" ("administration," NIV, 1 Cor. 12:28). As we noted before, even though the church is an organism, it must be organized or it will die. Leadership is a part of spiritual organization.

In this section, Paul described the bishop, the deacon, and the church itself. By understanding these three descriptions, we shall be able to give better leadership to the ministry of the church.

1. The pastor (1 Tim. 3:1-7)

According to the New Testament, the terms "bishop," "pastor," and "elder" are synonymous. "Bishop" means "overseer," and the elders had the responsibility of overseeing the work of the church (1 Peter 5:1-3; Acts 20:17, 28). "Elder" is the translation of the Greek word *presbutes*, which means "an old man." Paul used the word "presbytery" in 1 Timothy 4:14, referring not to a denomination, but to the "eldership" of the assembly that ordained Timothy. Elders and bishops (two names for the same office, Titus 1:5, 7) were mature people with spiritual wisdom and experience. Finally, "pastor" means "shepherd," one who leads and cares for the flock of God.

When you compare the qualifications given here for bishops with those given for elders in Titus 1:5-9, you quickly see that the same office is in view. Church organization was quite simple in apostolic days: There were pastors (elders, bishops) and deacons (Phil. 1:1). It seems that there was a plurality of elders overseeing the work of each church, some involved in "ruling" (organization and government), others in teaching (1 Tim. 5:17).

But these men had to be qualified. It was good for a growing believer to aspire to the office of bishop, but the best way to achieve it was to develop Christian character and meet the following requirements. To become an elder/bishop was a serious decision, one not treated lightly in the early church. Paul gave 16 qualifications for a man to meet if he expected to serve as an elder/bishop/pastor.

A. BLAMELESS (1 TIM. 3:2). This word literally means "nothing to take hold upon," that is, there must be nothing in his life that Satan or the unsaved can take hold of to criticize or attack the church. No man living is sinless, but we must strive to be blameless, or "above reproach" (NIV).

B. THE HUSBAND OF ONE WIFE (1 TIM. 3:2). All of the qualifying adjectives in this passage are masculine. While there is ample scope for feminine ministry in a local assembly, the office of elder is not given to women. However, a pastor's home life is very important, and especially his marital status. (This same requirement applies to deacons, per verse 12.) It means that a pastor must not be divorced and remarried. Paul was certainly not referring to polygamy, since no church member, let alone a pastor, would be accepted if he had more than one wife. Nor is he referring to remarriage after the death of the wife; for why would a pastor be prohibited from marrying again, in the light of Genesis 2:18 and 1 Timothy 4:3? Certainly the members of the church who had lost mates could marry again, so why penalize the pastor?

It's clear that a man's ability to manage his own marriage and home indicate ability to oversee a local church (1 Tim. 3:4-5). A pastor who has been divorced opens himself and the church to criticism from outsiders, and it is not likely that people with marital difficulties would consult a man who could not keep his own marriage together. I see no reason why *dedicated* Christians who have been divorced and remarried cannot serve in other offices in the church, but they are disqualified from being elders or deacons.

C. VIGILANT (1 Tim. 3:2). This means "temperate" or "sober." "Temperate in all things" (2 Tim. 4:5, literal translation). Or "keep your head in all situations" (NIV). A pastor needs to exercise sober, sensible judgment in all things.

D. SOBER (1 Tim. 3:2). He must have a serious attitude and be in earnest about his work. This does not mean he has no sense of humor, or that he is always solemn and somber. Rather it suggests that he knows the values of things and does not cheapen the ministry or the Gospel message by foolish behavior.

E. OF GOOD BEHAVIOR (1 Tim. 3:2). "Orderly" would be a good translation. The pastor should be organized in his thinking and his living, as well as in his teaching and preaching. It is the same Greek word that is translated "modest" in 1 Timothy 2:9, referring to women's clothing.

F. GIVEN TO HOSPITALITY (1 TIM. 3:2). Literally, "loving the stranger." This was an important ministry in the early church when traveling believers would need places to stay (Rom. 12:13; Heb. 13:2; 3 John 5-8). But even today, a pastor and wife who are hospitable are a great help to the fellowship of a local church.

G. APT TO TEACH (1 TIM. 3:2). Teaching the Word of God is one of an elder's main ministries. In fact, many scholars believe that "pastors and teachers" in Ephesians 4:11 refer to one person but to two functions. A pastor is automatically a teacher (2 Tim. 2:2, 24). Phillips Brooks, famous American preacher, has said, "Apt to teach—it is not something to which one comes by accident or by any sudden burst of fiery zeal." A pastor must be a careful student of the Word of God, and of all that assists him in knowing and teaching that Word. The pastor who is lazy in his study is a disgrace in the pulpit.

H. NOT GIVEN TO WINE (1 TIM. 3:3). The word describes a person who sits long with the cup and thus drinks to excess. The fact that Paul advised Timothy to use wine for medicinal purposes (5:23) indicates that total abstinence was not demanded of believers. Sad to say, some of the members of the Corinthian church got drunk, even at the love feast that accompanied the Lord's Supper! (1 Cor. 11:21) The Jewish people diluted their wine with water to make sure it was not too strong. It is a well-known fact that water was not pure in those days, so that weak wine taken in moderation would have been healthier to drink.

However, there is a vast difference between the cultural use of wine in Bible days and supporting the alcohol industry of today. Paul's admonition and example in Romans 14 (especially verse 21) would apply today in a special way. A godly pastor would certainly want to give the best example and not be an excuse for sin in the life of some weaker brother.

I. NO STRIKER (1 TIM. 3:3). "Not contentious, not looking for a fight." Charles Spurgeon told his Pastor's College students, "Don't go about the world with your fist doubled up for fighting, carrying a theological revolver in the leg of your trousers."

J. NOT GREEDY OF FILTHY LUCRE (1 TIM. 3:3). Paul will have more to say about money in 6:3ff. It is possible to use the ministry as an easy way to make money, if a man has no conscience or integrity. (Not that pastors are paid that much in most churches!) Covetous pastors always have "deals" going on outside their churches, and these activities erode their character and hinder their ministry. Pastors should "not [work] for filthy lucre" (1 Peter 5:2).

K. PATIENT (1 TIM. 3:3). "Gentle" is a better translation. The pastor must listen to people, be able to take criticism without reacting. He should permit others to serve God in the church without being "dictated to" by the pastor.

L. NOT A BRAWLER (1 TIM. 3:3). Pastors must be peacemakers, not troublemakers. This does not mean they must compromise their convictions, but that they must "disagree without being disagreeable." Short tempers do not make for long ministries.

M. NOT COVETOUS (1 TIM. 3:3). You can covet many things besides money: popularity, a large ministry that makes you famous, denominational advancement, etc. This word centers mainly on money.

N. A GODLY FAMILY (1 TIM. 3:4-5). This does not mean that a pastor must be married, or, if married, must have children. However, marriage and a family are probably in the will of God for most pastors. If a man's own children cannot obey and respect him, then his church is not likely to respect and obey his leadership. For Christians, the church and the home are one: We should oversee both of them with love, truth, and discipline. The pastor cannot be one thing at home and something else in church. If he is, his children will detect it, and there will be problems. The words "rule" and "ruleth" in verses 4 and 5 mean "to preside over, to govern," and suggest that a pastor is the one who directs the business of the church. (Not as a dictator, of course, but as a loving shepherd—1 Peter 5:3.) The word translated "take care of" in verse 5 suggests a personal ministry to the needs of the church. It is used in the parable of the Good Samaritan to describe the care given to the injured man (Luke 10:34-35).

O. NOT A NOVICE (1 TIM. 3:6). "Novice" literally means "one newly planted," referring to a young Christian. Age is no guarantee of maturity, but it is good for a man to give himself time for study and growth before he accepts a church. Some men mature faster than others, of course. Satan enjoys seeing a youthful pastor succeed, get proud, and then tear down all that has been built up.

P. A GOOD TESTIMONY OUTSIDE THE CHURCH (1 TIM. 3:7). Does he pay his bills? Does he have a good reputation among unsaved people with whom he does business? (See Col. 4:5 and 1 Thes. 4:12.)

No pastor ever feels that he is all he ought to be, and his people need to pray for him constantly. It is not easy to serve as a pastor/elder, but it is much easier if your character is all God wants it to be.

2. The deacon (1 Tim. 3:8-13)

The English word "deacon" is a transliteration of the Greek word *diakonos* which simply means "servant." It is likely that the origin of the deacons is recorded in Acts 6. The first deacons were appointed to be assistants to the apostles. In a local church today deacons relieve the pastors/elders of other tasks so that they may concentrate on the ministry of the Word, prayer, and spiritual oversight.

Even though deacons are not given the authority of elders, they still must meet certain qualifications. Many faithful deacons have been made elders after they proved themselves.

A. GRAVE (1 TIM. 3:8). A deacon should be worthy of respect; a man of Christian character worth imitating. A deacon should take his responsibilities seriously and *use* the office, not just *fill* it.

B. NOT DOUBLE-TONGUED (1 TIM. 3:8). He does not tell tales from house to house; he is not a gossip. He does not say one thing to one member and something entirely opposite to another member. You can depend on what he says.

C. NOT GIVEN TO MUCH WINE (1 TIM. 3:8). We have discussed this in our comments on verse 3.

D. NOT GREEDY OF FILTHY LUCRE (1 TIM. 3:8). Deacons handle offerings and distribute money to needy people in the church. It may be tempting to steal, or to use the funds in selfish ways. Finance committees in churches need to have a spiritual attitude toward money.

E. DOCTRINALLY SOUND (1 TIM. 3:9). The word "mystery" means "truth once hidden but now revealed by God." The great doctrines of the faith are hidden to those outside the faith, but they can be understood by those who trust the Lord. Deacons must understand

Christian doctrine and obey it with a good conscience. It is not enough to sit in meetings and decide how to "run the church." They must base their decisions on the Word of God, and they must back up their decisions with godly lives.

I have noticed that some church officers know their church constitutions better than they know the Word of God. While it is good to have by-laws and regulations that help maintain order, it is important to manage the affairs of a church on the basis of the Word of God. The Scriptures were the "constitution" of the early church! A deacon who does not know the Bible is an obstacle to progress in a local assembly.

A pastor friend of mine, now home with the Lord, took a church that was a split from another church and constantly at war with itself. From what he told me, their business meetings were something to behold! The church constitution was revered almost as much as the Bible. The people called it "the green book." My friend began to teach the people the Word of God, and the Spirit began to make changes in lives. But the enemy went to work and stirred up some officers to defy their pastor in a meeting.

"You aren't following the green book!" they said.

My friend lifted his Bible high and asked, "Are we going to obey the Word of God, or a green book written by men?" This was a turning point in the church, and then God blessed with wonderful growth and power.

A deacon who does not *know* the Word of God cannot manage the affairs of the church of God. A deacon who does not *live* the Word of God, but has a "defiled conscience," cannot manage the church of God. Simply because a church member is popular, successful in business, or generous in his giving does not mean he is qualified to serve as a deacon.

F. TESTED AND PROVED (1 TIM. 3:10). This implies watching their lives and seeing how they conduct themselves. In most churches, a new member or a new Christian may begin serving God in visitation, ushering, helping in Sunday School, and numerous other ways. This is the principle in Matthew 25:21: "Thou hast been faithful over a few things; I will make thee ruler over many things."

It is worth noting that quite a few leaders mentioned in the Bible were first tested as servants. Joseph was a servant in Egypt for 13 years before he became second ruler in the land. Moses cared for sheep for 40 years before God called him. Joshua was Moses' servant before he became Moses' successor. David was tending his father's sheep when Samuel invited him to be anointed king of Israel. Even our Lord Jesus came as a servant and labored as a carpenter; and the Apostle Paul was a tentmaker. First a servant, then a ruler.

It always weakens the testimony of a local church when a member who has not been proved is made an officer of the church. "Maybe Jim will attend church more if we make him a deacon," is a statement that shows ignorance both of Jim and of the Word of God. *An untested Christian is an unprepared Christian*. He will probably do more harm than good if you give him an office in the church.

G. GODLY HOMES (1 TIM. 3:11-12). The deacon's wife is a part of his ministry, for godliness must begin at home. The deacons must not be men who have been divorced and remarried. Their wives must be Christians, women who are serious about the ministry, not given to slanderous talk (literally "not devils," for the word "devil" means "slanderer, false accuser"), and faithful in all that they do. It is sad to see the damage that is done to a local church when the wives of elders or deacons gossip and slander others.

Some students think that verse 11 refers, not to the wives of the deacons, but to another order of ministers—the deaconesses. Many churches do have deaconesses who assist with the women's work, in baptisms, in fellowship times, etc. Phoebe was a deaconess in the church at Cenchrea (Rom. 16:1, where the word is *diakonon*). Perhaps in some of the churches, the wives of the deacons did serve as deaconesses. We thank God for the ministry of godly women in the local church, whether they hold offices or not! It is not necessary to hold an office to have a ministry or exercise a gift.

H. A WILLINGNESS TO WORK (1 TIM. 3:13). He is to *use* the office, not just *fill* it. The Greek word translated "degree" means "rank (as in the army), a base, a step, or a rung on a ladder." What an encouragement to a faithful deacon! God will "promote" him spiritually and give him more and more respect among the saints, which means greater opportunity for ministry. A faithful deacon has a good standing before God and men, and can be used of God to build the church. He has a spiritual boldness that makes for effective ministry.

Certainly a part of this blessing could include the possibility of "spiritual promotion." What a joy it is to a pastor to see deacons become elders, and then see some of the elders called into pastoral ministry on a full-time basis. (It should be remembered that, in the New Testament churches, the elders were called from out of their own local congregations. They were not imported from other places.)

It is a serious matter to serve in the local church. Each of us must search his own heart to be certain that he is qualified, by the grace of God.

3. The believers (1 Tim. 3:14-16)

Elders, deacons, and church members need to be reminded of what a local church is. In this brief paragraph, Paul gave three pictures of the church.

A. THE HOUSE OF GOD (1 TIM. 3:15). God's church is a family, so "household" might be a better translation. One of Paul's favorite words is "brethren" (see 4:6). When a sinner believes in Jesus Christ as Saviour, he immediately is born again into God's family (John 1:11-13; 1 Peter 1:22-25). Paul advised young Timothy to treat the members of the local church as he would treat the members of his own family (1 Tim. 5:1-2).

Because the local church is a family, it must be fed; and the only diet that will nourish the people is the Word of God. It is our bread (Matt. 4:4), milk and meat (1 Cor. 3:1-2; Heb. 5:12-14), and honey (Ps. 119:103). A pastor must take time to nourish himself so that he might nourish others (1 Tim. 4:6). A church does not grow by addition, but by nutrition (Eph. 4:11-16). It is tragic to see the way some pastors waste their time (and their church's time) all week long and then have nothing nourishing to give the people on the Lord's Day.

Like a family, a church needs discipline in love. Children who are not disciplined become rebels and tyrants. The spiritual leaders of the assembly should exercise discipline (1 Cor. 5 and 2 Cor. 2:6-11; 1 Cor. 4:18-21). Sometimes the children need rebuke; other times the discipline must be more severe.

Children also need encouragement and example (1 Thes. 2:7-12). Spiritual leaders must have the gentleness of a nursing mother and the strength of a loving father.

B. THE ASSEMBLY (1 TIM. 3:15). The word "church" is a translation of the Greek word *ekklēsia* (ek-klay-SEE-

a) which means "assembly." It referred to the political assemblies in the Greek cities (Acts 19:29, 32) where business was transacted by qualified citizens. But it is used about 100 times in the New Testament to refer to local churches, assemblies of believers. The Greek word means "those called out." (It is used in Acts 7:38 to describe the nation of Israel, called out of Egypt; but Israel was not a "church" in the New Testament sense.)

Paul wanted young Timothy to know how to "conduct himself" as a leader of a local assembly. The Pastoral Epistles are guidebooks for conduct of a local church. Scores of books have been published in recent years, purporting to tell us how to start, build, and increase a local church; and some of them contain good counsel. However, the best counsel for managing a local church is found in these three inspired letters. The young pastor in his first church, as well as the seasoned veteran in the ministry, should saturate himself with the teachings Paul shared with Timothy and Titus.

There are many different kinds of "assemblies," but the church is the assembly of the living God. Because it is God's assembly, He has the right to tell us how it ought to be governed. The church has been purchased with the blood of God's Son (Acts 20:28); therefore, we must be careful how we conduct ourselves. Church officers must not become religious dictators who abuse the people in order to achieve their own selfish ends (1 Peter 5:3-5 and 3 John 9-12).

C. THE PILLAR AND GROUND OF THE TRUTH (1 TIM. 3:15-16). This is an architectural image, and it would mean much to Timothy at Ephesus; for the great temple of Diana had 127 pillars. The word "ground" suggests a *bulwark* or a *stay*. The local church is built on

Jesus Christ the Truth (John 14:6; 1 Cor. 3:9-15); but the local church is also itself a pillar and bulwark for the truth.

It is likely that the *pillar* aspect of the church's ministry relates primarily to displaying the truth of the Word, much as a statue is put on a pedestal so all can see it. We must hold "forth the Word of life" so the world can see it (Phil. 2:16). The local church puts Jesus Christ on display in the lives of faithful members.

As a *bulwark*, the church protects the truth and makes sure it does not fall (for elsewhere "truth is fallen in the street, and equity cannot enter"—Isa. 59:14). When local churches turn away from the truth (1 Tim. 4:1ff) and compromise in their ministry, then the enemy makes progress. Sometimes church leaders must take a militant stand against sin and apostasy. This does not make them popular, but it does please the Lord.

The main truth to which a church should bear witness is the person and work of Jesus Christ (3:16—it is probable that this verse is quoted from an early Christian hymn). Jesus Christ was God *manifest in the flesh*, not only at His birth, but during His entire earthly ministry (John 14:1-9). Though His own people as a nation rejected Him, Jesus Christ was *vindicated in the Spirit*; for the Spirit empowered Him to do miracles and even to raise Himself from the dead (Rom. 1:4). The very presence of the Spirit in the world is itself a judgment on the world (John 16:7-11).

Seen of angels suggests the many times that the elect angels associated with the life and ministry of our Lord. (The word *angelos*, translated "angels," also means "messengers." See James 2:25. Perhaps Paul was referring to the chosen messengers who witnessed the resurrected Christ.) However, Christ did not die for angels, but for lost sinners; and so He was *preached unto the nations*. This reminds us of the commissions the Lord gave to His church to carry the Gospel to the ends of the earth, where He is *believed on in the world*. At the ascension, He was *received up in glory* (Acts 1:2, 22); and He will return one day to take His church to share that glory.

What an exciting challenge it is for your local church to witness of Jesus Christ to lost sinners at home, and around the world!

4
How to be a
Man of God

1 Timothy 4

If you were to write a job description for your pastor, what would it contain? How would it compare with the description he might write? We all know that a pastor preaches regularly, performs weddings and other Christian services, visits the sick, and counsels the distressed. But what *is* his ministry, and what kind of person must he be to fulfill his God-given ministry?

In this section of his letter to Timothy, Paul emphasized the character and the work of the minister himself; and he listed three qualities that a minister must possess if he is to be successful in serving God.

1. A good minister, preaching the Word (1 Tim. 4:1-6)

Paul had warned the Ephesian elders that false teachers would invade the church (Acts 20:28-31); and now they had arrived. The Holy Spirit had spoken in specific terms about these teachers, and the prophecy was starting to be fulfilled in Paul's time. Certainly it is fulfilled in our own time! We can recognize false teachers by the description Paul gave in this paragraph.

A. THEY ARE ENERGIZED BY SATAN (1 TIM. 4:1). This is the only place where demons are mentioned in the Pastoral Epistles. Just as there is a "mystery of godliness" concerning Christ (1 Tim. 3:16), so there is a "mystery of iniquity" that surrounds Satan and his work (2 Thes. 2:7). Satan is an imitator (2 Cor. 11:13-15); he has his own ministers and doctrines and seeks to deceive God's people and lead them astray (2 Cor. 11:3). The first test of any religious doctrine is what it says about Jesus Christ (1 John 4:1-6).

It comes as a shock to some people that Satan uses professed Christians *in the church* to accomplish his work. But Satan once used Peter to try to lead Jesus on a wrong path (Matt. 16:21-23), and he used Ananias and Sapphira to try to deceive the church at Jerusalem (Acts 5). Paul warned that false teachers would arise *from within the church* (Acts 20:30).

B. THEY LEAD PEOPLE ASTRAY (1 TIM. 4:1). Their goal is to seduce people and get them to depart from the faith. This is the word "apostasy," and it is defined as "a willful turning away from the truth of the Christian faith." These false teachers do not try to build up the church or relate people to the Lord Jesus Christ in a deeper way. Instead they want to get disciples to follow them and join their groups and promote their programs. This is one difference between a true church and a religious cult: A true church seeks to win converts to Jesus Christ and to build them spiritually; while a cult proselytizes, steals converts from others, and makes them servants (even slaves!) of the leaders of the cult. However, not all apostates are in cults; some of them are in churches *and pulpits*, teaching false doctrine and leading people astray.

C. THEY ARE HYPOCRITES (1 TIM. 4:2). "Ye shall know them by their fruits" (Matt. 7:15-20). These false teachers preach one thing but practice another. They tell their disciples what to do, but they do not do it themselves. Satan works "by means of the hypocrisy of liars" (literal translation, 1 Tim. 4:2). One of the marks of a true servant of God is his honesty and integrity: He practices what he preaches. This does not mean he is sinlessly perfect, but that he sincerely seeks to obey the Word of God. He tries to maintain a good conscience (see 1:5 and 19, and 3:9).

The word "seared" means "cauterized." Just as a person's flesh can be "branded" so that it becomes hard and without feeling, so a person's conscience can be deadened. Whenever we affirm with our lips something that we deny with our lives (whether people know it or not), we deaden our consciences just a little more. Jesus made it clear that it is not religious talk or even performing miracles that qualifies a person for heaven, but doing God's will in everyday life (Matt. 7:21-29).

An apostate is not just wrong doctrinally; he is wrong morally. His personal life became wrong before his doctrines were changed. In fact, it is likely that he changed his teachings so that he could continue his sinful living and pacify his conscience. *Believing* and *behaving* always go together.

D. THEY DENY GOD'S WORD (1 TIM. 4:3-5). The false teachers in Ephesus combined Jewish legalism with Eastern asceticism. You find Paul dealing with this same false doctrine in his letter to the Colossians (2:8-23 especially). For one thing, they taught that an unmarried life was more spiritual than a married life, which is contrary to Scripture. "It is not good that the man should be alone," are God's own words (Gen.

2:18). Jesus put His seal of approval on marriage (Matt. 19:1-9), though He pointed out that not everybody is supposed to marry (19:10-12). Paul also affirmed the biblical basis for marriage (1 Cor. 7:1-24), teaching that each person should follow the will of God in the matter.

Beware of any religious teaching that tampers with God's institution of marriage. And beware of any teaching that tampers with God's Creation. The false teachers who were infecting the Ephesian church taught that certain foods were taboo; if you ate them, you were not spiritual. The fact that God called His own Creation "good" (Gen. 1:10, 12, 18, 21, 25) did not interest these teachers. Their authority to dictate diets gave them power over their converts.

Those who "believe and know the truth" are not impressed with the do's and don'ts of the legalists. Jesus stated that all foods are clean (Mark 7:14-23). He taught this lesson again to Peter (Acts 10), and reaffirmed it through Paul (1 Cor. 10:23-33). A person may not be able to eat certain foods for physical reasons (an allergy, for example); but no food is to be rejected for spiritual reasons. We should not, however, use our freedom to eat and drink to destroy weaker Christians (Rom. 14:13-23). The food we eat is sanctified (set apart, devoted to God) when we pray and give thanks; so the Word of God and prayer turn even an ordinary meal into a spiritual service for God's glory (1 Cor. 10:31).

The emphasis in a minister's life should be on "the Word of God and prayer" (1 Tim. 4:5). It is tragic when a church keeps its pastors so busy with menial tasks that they have hardly any time for God's Word and prayer (Acts 6:1-7). Paul reminded young Timothy of his great responsibility to study, teach, and preach the

Scriptures, and to spend time in prayer. As a "good minister" he must be "nourished up in the words of faith" (1 Tim. 4:6). Timothy had certain responsibilities in the light of this growing apostasy.

E. TEACH THE CHURCH THE TRUTH (1 TIM. 4:6A). God's people need to be warned about false doctrine and religious apostasy. A minister must not major on these subjects, because he is obligated to teach "all the counsel of God" (Acts 20:27); but neither should he ignore them. As we travel the streets and highways, we see two kinds of signs: those that tell us where we are going ("Boston 45 miles") and those that warn us of possible dangers ("Bridge Out!"). A pastor must teach positive doctrine so that people will know what they believe and where they are going. But he must also expose false doctrine so that people will not be seduced and led astray.

F. HE MUST NOURISH HIMSELF IN THE WORD (1 TIM. 4:6B). Of course, *every* Christian ought to feed daily on the Word (Matt. 4:4; 1 Peter 2:2; Jer. 15:16); but it is especially important that a pastor grow in the Word. It is by daily studying the "good doctrine" and meditating on the Word that he grows in the Lord and is able to lead the church.

The "good minister" preaches the Word that he himself feeds on day by day. But it is not enough to preach the Word; he must also practice it.

2. A godly minister, practicing the Word (1 Tim. 4:7-12)

Paul shifted into an athletic illustration at this point in his letter. Just as a Greek or Roman athlete had to refuse certain things, eat the right food, and do the right exercises, so a Christian should practice "spiritual exercise." If a Christian puts as much energy and discipline into his spiritual life as an athlete does into his game, the Christian grows faster and accomplishes much more for God. Paul discussed in this section three levels of life:

A. THE BAD—"PROFANE AND OLD WIVES' FABLES" (1 TIM. 4:7A). These are, of course, the false teachings and traditions of the apostates. These doctrines have no basis in Scripture; in fact, they contradict the Word of God. They are the kind of teachings that silly people would discuss, not dedicated men and women of the Word! No doubt these teachings involved the false doctrines just named (4:2-3). Paul also warned Titus about "Jewish fables" (Titus 1:14). Paul warned Timothy about these same "fables" in his second letter (2 Tim. 4:4).

A believer cannot discover new doctrines. Paul admonished Timothy to remain true to "the good doctrine which you have closely followed up to now" (4:6b, literal translation). He warned him not to "give heed to fables and endless genealogies" (1 Tim. 1:4). While a pastor must know what the enemy is teaching, he must not be influenced by it. A chemist may handle and study poisons, but he does not permit them to get into his system.

B. THE TEMPORARY "BODILY EXERCISE" (1 TIM. 4:7-8). Again, this is an athletic image. Certainly we ought to care for our bodies, and exercise is a part of that care. Our bodies are God's temples, to be used for His glory (1 Cor. 6:19-20), and His tools for His service (Rom. 12:1-2). But bodily exercise benefits us only during this life; godly exercise is profitable now and for eternity. Paul did not ask Timothy to choose between the two; I think God expects us to practice both. A healthy body can be used of God, but we must major on holiness.

C. The eternal—"godliness" (1 Tim. 4:7-8). Phillips Brooks said, "The great purpose of life—the shaping of character by truth." Godly character and conduct are far more important than golf trophies or home-run records, though it is possible for a person to have both. Paul challenged Timothy to be as devoted to godliness as an athlete is to his sport. We are living and laboring for eternity.

Paul used two similar athletic images in writing to the Corinthians (1 Cor. 9:24-27), emphasizing the disciplines necessary for godly living. As an athlete must control his body and obey the rules, so a Christian must make his body his servant and not his master. When I see high school football squads and baseball teams, under the hot summer sun, going through their calisthenics, I am reminded that there are spiritual exercises that I ought to be doing (Heb. 5:14). Prayer, meditation, self-examination, fellowship, service, sacrifice, submission to the will of others, witness—all of these can assist me, through the Spirit, to become a more godly person.

Spiritual exercise is not easy; we must "labor and suffer reproach" (1 Tim. 4:10a). "For this we labor and strive" (niv). The word translated "strive" is an athletic word from which we get our English word "agonize." It is the picture of an athlete straining and giving his best to win. A Christian who wants to excel must really work at it, by the grace of God and to the glory of God.

But exercising ourselves in godly living is not only profitable for us; it is also profitable for others (4:11-12). It enables us to be good examples, so that we encourage others. Paul named several areas of life in which you and I should be examples.

In word (4:12) implies that our speech should always

be honest and loving, "speaking the truth in love" (Eph. 4:15).

In conduct (the kjv's "conversation" means "walk," not "talk") suggests that our lives are to be controlled by the Word of God. We must not be like the hypocrites Paul described to Titus (1:16): "They profess that they know God; but in works they deny Him."

In love (charity) points to the motivation of our lives. We do not obey God to be applauded by men (Matt. 6:1ff), but because we love God and love God's people.

(*In spirit* is not in many manuscripts, but it would describe the inner enthusiasm and excitement of a child of God.)

In faith implies that we trust God and are faithful to Him. Faith and love often go together (1 Tim. 1:14; 2:15; 6:11; 2 Tim. 1:13; 2:22). Faith always leads to faithfulness.

In purity is important as we live in this present evil world. Ephesus was a center for sexual impurity, and the young man Timothy was faced with temptations. He must have a chaste relationship to the women in the church (1 Tim. 5:2) and keep himself pure in mind, heart, and body.

But godly living not only helps *us* and *other believers*; it also has its influence on *the lost*. Paul reminded pastor Timothy that Jesus Christ is the Saviour (4:10), and it is the believer's task to share that Good News with the lost. In effect he wrote, "We Christians have fixed our hope in the living God, but the lost have no hope and do not know the living God. All that many of them know are the dead idols that can never save them."

The title "Saviour of all men" does not imply that everybody will be saved (universalism), or that God saves people in spite of themselves; for Paul added "specially of those that believe." It is faith that saves one's soul (Eph. 2:8-10). Since God "will have all men to be saved" (1 Tim. 2:4), and since Christ "gave Himself a ransom for all" (2:6), then *any* lost sinner can trust Christ and be saved. Christ is "the Saviour of all men," so nobody need despair.

Timothy should not fear to practice the Word of God and apply it to the life of the church, for this Word is "a faithful saying and worthy of all acceptation" (4:9). These faithful sayings made up a summary of truth for the early church (see 1:15; 3:1; 2 Tim. 2:11; Titus 3:8). The fact that Timothy was a young man (the word then applied to a person from youth to 40) should not deter him from practicing the Word. In fact, he was to "command" these things, and this is our military word "charge" (1 Tim. 1:3). The local church is a unit in God's spiritual army, and its leaders are to pass God's orders along to the people with authority and conviction.

3. A growing minister, progressing in the Word (1 Tim. 4:13-16)

The key thought in this section is "that thy profiting may appear to all" (4:15). The word "profiting" ("progress," NIV) is a Greek military term; it means "pioneer advance." It describes the soldiers who go ahead of the troops, clear away the obstacles, and make it possible for others to follow. As a godly pastor, Timothy was to grow spiritually so that the whole church could see his spiritual progress and imitate it.

No pastor can lead his people where he has not been himself. "Such as I have, give I thee" is a basic principle of life and ministry (Acts 3:6). The pastor (or church member) who is not growing is actually going backward, for it is impossible to stand still in the Christian life. In his living, teaching, preaching, and leading, the minister must give evidence of spiritual growth. But what are factors that make spiritual progress possible?

A. Emphasize God's Word (1 Tim. 4:13). "Give attendance to" means "devote yourself to, be absorbed in." The minister of the Word was not something Timothy was to do after he had done other things; it was to be the most important thing he did. *Reading* means the public reading of Scripture in the local assembly. The Jewish people always had the reading of the Law and the Prophets in their synagogues, and this practice carried over into Christian churches. Jesus read the Scriptures in the synagogue at Nazareth (Luke 4:16ff), and Paul often read the lessons when he visited a synagogue (Acts 13:15).

In my itinerant ministry, I have noted that many churches have dispensed with the public reading of God's Word; and I am disappointed. They have time for "special music" and endless announcements, but there is no time for the reading of the Bible. The pastor may read a text before he preaches, but that is a different thing. Every local church ought to have a schedule of Bible readings for the public services. It is commanded by Scripture that we read God's Word in the public assemblies. (I might add that those who read the Word publicly ought to prepare themselves privately. Nobody should be asked "at the last minute" to read the Scriptures publicly. The Bible deserves the best we can give.)

Exhortation (1 Tim. 4:13) literally means "encouragement" and suggests the applying of the Word to the lives of the people. The pastor was to read the Word, explain it, and apply it. *Doctrine* means "teaching," and is a major emphasis in the pastoral letters. There are at least 22 references to "teaching" or "doctrine" in these 13 chapters.

"Apt to teach" is one of the qualifications of a minister (1 Tim. 3:2); and it has been correctly said, "Apt to teach implies apt to learn." A growing minister (or church member) must be a student of the Word. Before he teaches others he teaches himself (Rom. 2:21). His spiritual progress is an example to his flock and an encouragement to others.

B. USE YOUR SPIRITUAL GIFTS (1 TIM. 4:14). So much has been written in recent years about spiritual gifts that we have almost forgotten the *graces* of the Spirit (Gal. 5:22-23). The word "gift" is the Greek word *charisma*. It simply means "a gracious gift from God." (The world uses the word "charisma" to describe a person with magnetic personality and commanding appearance.) *Every Christian* has the gift of the Spirit (Rom. 8:9) and at least one gift from the Spirit (1 Cor. 12:1-11). The gift of the Spirit, and the gifts from the Spirit, are bestowed by God at the moment of conversion (see 1 Cor. 12:13ff).

However, when God calls a believer into a special place of ministry, He can (and often does) impart a spiritual gift for that task. When Timothy was ordained by the elders ("presbytery"), he received an enabling gift from God when the elders laid hands on him. But for some reason, Timothy had neglected to cultivate this gift which was so necessary to his spiritual progress and ministry. In fact, Paul had to admonish him in his second letter, "Stir up the gift of God, which is in thee by the putting on of my hands" (2 Tim. 1:6).

It is encouraging to know that the God who calls us also equips us to do His work. We have nothing in ourselves that enables us to serve Him; the ministry must all come from God (1 Cor. 15:9-10; 1 Tim. 1:12;

Phil. 4:13). However, we must not be passive; we must cultivate God's gifts, use them, and develop them, in the ministry of the local church and wherever God puts us.

C. Devote yourself fully to Christ (1 Tim. 4:15). "Meditate" carries the idea of "be in them, give yourself totally to them." Timothy's spiritual life and ministry were to be the absorbing, controlling things in his life, not merely sidelines that he occasionally practiced. There can be no real pioneer advance in one's ministry unless there is total dedication to the task. "No man can serve two masters" (Matt. 6:24).

While I do not want to sound critical, I must confess that I am disturbed by the fact that too many pastors and Christian workers divide their time and interest between the church and some sideline. It may be real estate, trips to the Holy Land, politics, civic duties, even denominational service. Their own spiritual lives suffer, and their churches suffer, because these men are not devoting themselves wholly to their ministry. "This one thing I do" was Paul's controlling motive, and it ought to be ours too (Phil. 3:13). "A double-minded man is unstable in all his ways" (James 1:8).

D. Take spiritual inventory (1 Tim. 4:16). Examine your own heart in the light of the Word of God. Note that Paul put "thyself" ahead of "the doctrine." Paul had given this same warning to the Ephesian elders in his farewell message: "Take heed therefore unto yourselves" (Acts 20:28). A servant of God can be so busy helping others that he neglects himself and his own spiritual walk.

The great American evangelist Charles Finney used to preach a sermon on this text. He titled it, "Preacher, Save Thyself!" That sermon is needed today, for we are seeing people having to leave the ministry because their lives have not kept up with their profession. Moral problems, divorces, and other kinds of shameful conduct have destroyed many of God's servants. "Let him that thinketh he standeth take heed lest he fall" (1 Cor. 10:12).

The building up of the saved, and the winning of the lost, are the purposes for our ministry, to the glory of God. But God must work *in* us before He can effectively work *through* us (Phil. 2:12-13). As good ministers, we preach the Word; as godly ministers, we practice the Word; as growing ministers, we progress in the Word.

5
Order in the Church!

1 Timothy 5

The first problem the early church faced was also a modern one: A group of church members was neglected by the ministering staff (Acts 6). I once heard a certain pastor described as "a man who is invisible during the week, and incomprehensible on Sunday." Again, somebody in his congregation was feeling neglected.

Then Paul instructed Timothy how to minister to specific groups in his church.

1. The older members (1 Tim. 5:1-2)

Paul admonished Timothy to minister to the various kinds of people in the church, and not to show partiality (1 Tim. 5:21). Since Timothy was a younger man, he might be tempted to ignore the older members; so Paul urged him to love and serve all of the people, regardless of their ages. The church is a family: Treat the older members like your mother and father, and the younger members like your brothers and sisters.

2. The older widows (1 Tim. 5:3-10)

From the beginning of its ministry, the church had a concern for believing widows (Acts 6:1; 9:39). Of course, the nation of Israel had sought to care for widows; and God had given special legislation to protect them (Deut. 10:18; 24:17; Isa. 1:17). God's special care for the widows is a recurring theme in Scripture (Deut. 14:29; Ps. 94:6; Mal. 3:5). It was only right that the local church show compassion to these women who were in need.

However, the church must be careful not to waste its resources on people who really are not in need. Whether we like to admit it or not, there are individuals and entire families that milk local churches, while they themselves refuse to work or to use their own resources wisely. As long as they can get handouts from the church, why bother to go to work?

Paul listed the qualifications a widow must meet if she is to be supported by the church.

A. WITHOUT HUMAN SUPPORT (1 TIM. 5:5A, "DESOLATE"). If a widow had relatives they should care for her so that the church might use its money to care for others who have no help. If her own children were dead, then her grandchildren (the KJV translates them "nephews" in verse 4) should accept the responsibility. When you recall that society in that day did not have the kind of institutions we have today—pensions, Social Security, retirement homes, etc.—you can see how important family care really was. Of course, the presence of such institutions *today* does not relieve any family of its loving obligations. "Honor thy father and thy mother" is still in the Bible (Ex. 20:12; Eph. 6:1-3).

Suppose a relative is unwilling to help support his loved-one? "He . . . is worse than an unbeliever!" was

Paul's judgment (1 Tim. 5:8, NIV; also see verse 16). A missionary friend of mine, now with the Lord, came home from the field to care for her sick and elderly parents. She was severely criticized by some of her associates ("We should love God more than father and mother!"), but she remained faithful to the end. Then she returned to the field for years of fruitful service, knowing she had obeyed God. After all, we love God by loving His people; and He has a special concern for the elderly, the widows, and the orphans.

B. A BELIEVER WITH A FAITHFUL TESTIMONY (1 TIM. 5:5B). The church could not care for *all* the widows in the city, but it should care for believers who are a part of the fellowship. We should "do good unto all . . . especially unto them who are of the household of faith" (Gal. 6:10). A widow the church helps should not be a self-indulgent person, seeking pleasure, but a godly woman who hopes in God and has a ministry of intercession and prayer. See Luke 2:36-37 for an example of a godly widow.

It has been my experience in three different pastorates that godly widows are a "spiritual power-house" in the church. They are the backbone of the prayer meetings. They give themselves to visitation, and they swell the ranks of teachers in the Sunday School. It has also been my experience that, if a widow is *not* godly, she can be a great problem to the church. She will demand attention, complain about what the younger people do, and often "hang on the telephone" and gossip. (Of course, it is not really "gossip." She only wants her friends to be able to "pray more intelligently" about these matters!) Paul made it clear (1 Tim. 5:7) that church-helped widows must be "blameless"—irreproachable.

C. AT LEAST 60 YEARS OLD (1 TIM. 5:9A). A woman of

this age was not likely to get remarried in that day, though 60 is not considered that "old" today. Perhaps the verb "taken into the number" gives us a clue. It literally means "to be enrolled and put on the list." The word was used for the enrollment of soldiers. The early church had an official list of the names of qualified widows, and we get the impression that these "enlisted" women ministered to the congregation in various ways. (Remember Dorcas and her widow friends, Acts 9:36-43?) Paul probably would have told us if they had been officially ordained as deaconesses.

D. A GOOD MARRIAGE RECORD (1 TIM. 5:9). We have met this same requirement before, for bishops (3:2) and for deacons (3:12). The implication is that the widow was not a divorced woman. Since younger widows were advised to remarry (5:14), this stipulation cannot refer to a woman who had a temporary second marriage after the death of her husband. Faithfulness to one's marriage vows is very important in the eyes of God.

E. A WITNESS OF GOOD WORKS (1 TIM. 5:10). If a person is faithfully serving God, his light will shine and others will see it and glorify God (Matt. 5:16). "Brought up children" can refer either to her own children, or to orphans who needed a home. If it refers to her own children, then they would have to have died; otherwise the church would not support her. It is likely that the reference here is to the practice of rescuing abandoned children and raising them to know the Lord.

Hospitality is another factor, for this was an important ministry in those days when travel was dangerous and safe places to sleep were scarce. The washing of feet does not refer to a special ritual, but to the common practice of washing a guest's feet when he arrived in the home (Luke 7:44). It was not beneath this woman's dignity to take the place of a humble servant.

"Relieved the afflicted" could cover many kinds of ministry to the needy: feeding the hungry, caring for the sick, encouraging the sorrowing, etc. Every pastor gives thanks for godly women who minister to the material and physical needs in the church. These widows were cared for by the church, but they, in turn, helped to care for the church.

3. The younger widows (1 Tim. 5:11-16)

The younger widows would technically be women under 60 years of age, but no doubt Paul had much younger women in mind. It was not likely that a 59-year-old woman would "bear children" if she remarried! (5:14) The dangers of travel, the ravages of disease, war, and a host of other things could rob a young wife of her husband. But Paul forbade Timothy to enroll the younger widows and put them under the care of the church.

A. THE REASONS FOR REFUSING THEM (1 TIM. 5:11-14). Because of their age, younger widows are naturally attracted to men and want to marry again. What is so bad about that? Paul seems to imply (5:12) that each of the widows enrolled pledged herself to remain a widow and serve the Lord in the church. This pledge must not be interpreted as a "vow of celibacy," nor should we look on this group of ministering widows as a "special monastic order." There seemed to be an agreement between the widows and the church that they would remain widows and serve the Lord.

There is another possible interpretation: These younger widows, if supported by the church, would have opportunities to "live it up" and find other husbands, most likely unbelievers. By marrying an unbeliever, they would be casting off their first faith. However, I prefer the first explanation.

Paul does make it clear (5:13) that younger widows, if cared for by the church, would have time on their hands and get involved in sinful activities. They would get in the habit of being idle instead of being useful. They would gad about from house to house and indulge in gossip and be busybodies. There is a definite connection between idleness and sin.

Paul warned Timothy against using the "charity" ministry of the church to encourage people to be idle. The church certainly ought to assist those who really need help, but it must not subsidize sin. As a pastor, I have had to make decisions in these matters, and sometimes it is not easy.

B. REQUIREMENTS FOR YOUNGER WIDOWS (1 TIM. 5:14-16). From the negative, Paul listed the positive things he wanted the younger widows to do, to be accepted and approved in the church. He wanted the younger widows to marry and have families. While not every person is supposed to get married, marriage is natural for most people who have been married before. Why remain in lonely widowhood if there was yet opportunity for a husband and a family? Of course, all of this would have to be "in the Lord" (1 Cor. 7:39).

"Be fruitful and multiply" was God's mandate to our first parents (Gen. 1:28), so the normal result of marriage is a family. Those today who refuse to have children because of the "awfulness of the times" should check out how difficult the times were in Paul's day! If *Christians* do not have children and raise them to live for God, who will?

"Guide the house" (1 Tim. 5:14) literally means "rule the house." The wife should manage the affairs of the household, and her husband should trust her to do so (Prov. 31:10-31). Of course, marriage is a partnership; but each partner has a special sphere of responsibility. Few men can do in a home what a woman can do. Whenever my wife has been ill, or has been caring for our babies, and I have had to manage some of the affairs of the home, I have discovered quickly that I was out of my sphere of ministry!

The result of all of this is a good testimony that silences the accusers. Satan (the adversary) is always alert to an opportunity to invade and destroy a Christian home. The word "occasion" is a military term that means "a base of operations." A Christian wife who is not doing her job at home gives Satan a beachhead for his operations, and the results are tragic. While there are times when a Christian wife and mother may have to work outside the home, the normal pattern is that she minister in the home. The wife who works simply to get luxuries may discover too late that she has lost some necessities. It may be all right to have what money can buy, *if* you do not lose what money cannot buy.

How Christian wives and mothers manage their homes can be a testimony to those outside the church. Much as a pastor is to have a good reputation with outsiders (3:7), and the servants are not to bring reproach on God's Word (6:1), so the wives are to have a good witness. Women may not be able to be elders of the church, but they can minister for the Lord right in their own homes. (See Titus 2:4-5 for an additional emphasis on this vital ministry.)

Paul then summarized the principle of each family caring for the needs of its own members (1 Tim. 5:16). Paul did not tell them *how* these widows should be relieved—giving them a regular dole, taking them into a home, giving them employment, etc. Each local assembly would have to decide this according to the needs of individual cases.

How does this principle apply to Christians today? Certainly we must honor our parents and grandparents and seek to provide for them if they have needs. Not every Christian family is able to take in another member, and not every widow wants to live with her children. Where there is sickness or handicap, professional care is necessary, and perhaps this cannot be given in a home. Each family must decide what God's will is in the matter, and no decision is easy. The important thing is that believers show love and concern and do all they can to help each other.

4. Church officers (1 Tim. 5:17-25)

The instructions in this section deal primarily with the elders, but the principles also apply to a pastor's relationship with any officer in his church. It is a wonderful thing when the elders and deacons (and other officers) work together in harmony and love. It is tragic when a pastor tries to become a spiritual dictator (1 Peter 5:3), or when an officer tries to be a preeminent big shot (3 John 9-10).

Apparently Timothy was having some problems with the elders of the church at Ephesus. He was a young man and still had much to learn. Ephesus was not an easy place to minister. Furthermore, Timothy had followed Paul as overseer of the church, and Paul would not be an easy man to follow! Paul's farewell address to the Ephesian elders (Acts 20) shows how hard he had worked and how faithful he had been, and how much the elders loved Paul (20:36-38). In spite of the fact that Paul had personally sent Timothy to Ephesus, the young man was having a hard time.

This situation may be the reason for Paul's instruction about wine (1 Tim. 5:23). Did Timothy have stomach trouble? Was he ill because of his many responsibilities and problems? Or had he tried to follow the ideas of some of the ascetics (4:1-5), only to discover that his diet was making him worse instead of better? We do not know the answers to all these questions; we can only read between the lines. It is worth noting that Paul's mention of wine here is not an endorsement of the entire alcohol industry. Using wine for medicinal reasons is not an encouragement for social drinking. As we have seen, though the Bible does not demand total abstinence, it does denounce drunkenness.

Paul counseled Timothy in his relationship to the elders by discussing three topics:

A. PAYING THE ELDERS (1 TIM. 5:17-18). In the early church, instead of one pastor, several elders ministered to the people. These men would devote themselves full time to the work of the Lord, and therefore they deserved some kind of remuneration. In most congregations today, the elders are laymen who have other vocations, but who assist in the work of the church. Usually the pastoral staff are the only full-time workers in the church. (Of course, there are also secretaries, custodians, etc., but Paul was not writing about them.)

There were two kinds of elders in the church: *ruling elders* who supervised the work of the congregation; and *teaching elders* who taught the Word of God. These elders were chosen from the congregation on the basis of God's call, the Spirit's equipping, and the witness and work of the men themselves. After they were chosen, they were ordained and set apart for this ministry (Acts 14:23; 20:17, 28; Titus 1:5).

The local church needs both ruling and teaching. The Spirit does give the gifts of "helps" and "governments" to the church (1 Cor. 12:28). If a church is not organized, there will be wasted effort, money, and opportunities. If spiritually minded leaders do not supervise the various ministries of the local church, there will be chaos instead of order. However, this supervision must not be dictatorial. You do not manage the work of a local church in the same manner as you do a grocery store or a manufacturing plant. While a church should follow good business principles, it is not a business. The ruthless way some church leaders have pushed people around is a disgrace to the Gospel.

But ruling without teaching would accomplish very little. The local church grows through the ministry of the Word of God (Eph. 4:11ff). You cannot rule over babies! Unless the believers are fed, cleansed, and strengthened by the Word, they will be weak and useless and will only create problems.

Paul told Timothy to be sure that the leaders were paid adequately, on the basis of their ministries. He quoted an Old Testament law to prove his point (Deut. 25:4). (The best commentary on this is 1 Cor. 9:7-14.) Then Paul added a statement from our Lord Jesus Christ: "The laborer deserves his wages" (Luke 10:7, NIV). This was a common saying in that day, but Paul equated the words of Christ with Old Testament Scripture!

If pastors are faithful in feeding and leading the people, then the church ought to be faithful and pay them adequately. "Double honor" (1 Tim. 5:17) can be translated "generous pay." (The word "honor" is used as in "honorarium.") It is God's plan that the needs of His servants be met by their local churches; and He will bless churches that are faithful to His servants. If a church is not faithful, and its pastor's needs are not met, it is a poor testimony; and God has ways of dealing with the situation. He can provide through other means, but then the church misses the blessing; or He may move His servant elsewhere.

The other side of the coin is this: A pastor must never minister simply to earn money (see 3:3). To "negotiate" with churches, or to canvass around looking for a place with a bigger salary, is not in the will of God. Nor is it right for a pastor to bring into his sermons his own financial needs, hoping to arouse some support from the finance committee!

B. DISCIPLINING THE ELDERS (1 TIM. 5:19-21). Church discipline usually goes to one of two extremes. Either there is no discipline at all, and the church languishes because of disobedience and sin. Or the church officers become evangelical policemen who hold a kangaroo court and violate many of the Bible's spiritual principles.

The disciplining of church *members* is explained in Matthew 18:15-18, 2 Thessalonians 3:6-16, 2 Timothy 2:23-26, Romans 16:17-18, 2 John 9-11, Galatians 6:1-3, Titus 3:10, 1 Corinthians 5, and 2 Corinthians 2:6-11.

Paul in this passage (1 Tim. 5:19-21) discussed the disciplining of church *leaders*. It is sad when a church member must be disciplined, but it is even sadder when a spiritual leader fails and must be disciplined; for leaders, when they fall, have a way of affecting others.

The purpose of discipline is restoration and not revenge. Our purpose must be to save the offender, not to drive him away. Our attitude must be one of love and tenderness (Gal. 6:1-3). In fact the verb "restore" that Paul used in Galatians 6:1 means "to set a broken bone." Think of the patience and tenderness involved in that procedure!

Paul's first caution to Timothy was to *be sure of his facts*, and the way to do that is to have witnesses (1 Tim. 5:19). This principle is also stated in Deuteronomy 19:15, Matthew 18:16, and 2 Corinthians 13:1. I think a dual application of the principle is suggested here. First, those who make any accusation against a pastor must be able to support it with witnesses. Rumor and suspicion are not adequate grounds for discipline. Second, when an accusation is made, witnesses ought to be present. In other words, the accused has the right to face his accuser in the presence of witnesses.

A church member approached me at a church dinner one evening, and began to accuse me of ruining the church. She had all sorts of miscellaneous bits of gossip, none of which was true. As soon as she started her tirade, I asked two of the officers standing nearby to witness what she was saying. Of course, she immediately stopped talking and marched defiantly away.

It is sad when churches disobey the Word and listen to rumors, lies, and gossip. Many a godly pastor has been defeated in his life and ministry in this way, and some have even resigned from the ministry. "Where there's smoke, there's fire" may be a good slogan for a volunteer fire department, but it does not apply to local churches. "Where there's smoke, there's fire" could possibly mean that somebody's tongue has been "set on fire of hell"! (James 3:6)

Paul's second caution was that Timothy do everything openly and aboveboard. The under-the-counter politics of city hall have no place in a church. "In secret have I said nothing," said Jesus (John 18:20). If an officer *is* guilty, then he should be rebuked before all the other leaders (1 Tim. 5:20). He should be given opportunity to repent, and if he does he should be forgiven (2 Cor. 2:6-11). Once he is forgiven, the matter is settled and should never be brought up again.

Paul's third caution (1 Tim. 5:21) is that Timothy obey the Word no matter what his personal feelings might be. He should act without prejudice *against* or partiality *for* the accused officer. There are no seniority rights in a local church; each member has the same standing before God and His Word. To show either prejudice or partiality is to make the situation even worse.

C. SELECTING AND ORDAINING THE ELDERS (1 TIM. 5:22-25). Only God knows the hearts of everyone (Acts 1:24). The church needs spiritual wisdom and guidance in selecting its officers. It is dangerous to impulsively place a new Christian or a new church member in a place of spiritual responsibility. Some people's sins are clearly seen; others are able to cover their sins, though their sins pursue them (1 Tim. 5:24). The good works of dedicated believers ought to be evident, even though they do not serve in order to be seen by people (5:25).

In other words, the church must carefully investigate the lives of potential leaders, to make sure that there is nothing seriously wrong. To ordain elders with sin in their lives is to partake of those sins! If simply saying "Good-bye" (God be with you) to a heretic makes us partakers of his evil deeds (2 John 10-11), then how much more guilty are we if we ordain people whose lives are not right with God?

No pastor or church member is perfect, but that should not hinder us from striving for perfection. The ministry of a local church rises and falls with its leadership. Godly leadership means God's blessing, and that is what we want and need.

6
Orders from Headquarters

1 Timothy 6

This chapter continues Paul's advice to Timothy on ministering to the various kinds of believers in the church. The atmosphere is military, for Paul used words that belong to the army: "Fight the good fight of faith" (6:12). "I give thee charge" (6:13, which is the same military term used in 1:3). "Charge them that are rich" (6:17). "O Timothy, keep [guard] that which is committed to thy trust" (6:20). In other words, you might say Paul was the general, giving Timothy orders from the Lord, the Commander-in-Chief.

D. L. Moody did not like his soloist, Ira Sankey, to use "Onward Christian Soldiers" in their evangelistic campaigns. Moody felt that the church he saw was very *un*like an army. If the average military man on our side in World War II had behaved toward his superiors and their orders the way the average Christian behaves toward the Lord, we probably would have lost the war! Instead of "Onward Christian Soldiers," someone has suggested that perhaps we ought to sing "Backward Christian Soldiers."

Paul instructed Timothy how to minister to three more groups in the church, and also how to keep his own life in the will of God.

1. Christian slaves (1 Tim. 6:1-2)

Some historians have estimated that half of the population of the Roman Empire was composed of slaves. Many of these people were educated and cultured, but legally they were not considered persons at all. The Gospel message of salvation and freedom in Christ appealed to the slaves, and many of them became believers. (The word translated "servant" in the KJV New Testament usually means "slave.") When slaves were able to get away from their household duties, they would fellowship in local assemblies where being a slave was not a handicap (Gal. 3:28).

But there was a problem: Some slaves used their new-found freedom in Christ as an excuse to disobey, if not defy, their masters. They needed to learn that their spiritual freedom in Christ did not alter their social position, even though they were accepted graciously into the fellowship of the church.

A. SLAVES WITH UNBELIEVING MASTERS (1 TIM. 6:1). No Christian master would consider his slaves "under the yoke," but would treat them with love and respect (Col. 4:1; Phile. 16). For a slave to rebel against an unsaved master would bring disgrace on the Gospel. "The name of God" and His doctrine would be blasphemed (Rom. 2:24). This is one reason Paul and the early missionaries did not go around preaching against the sinful institution of slavery. Such a practice would have branded the church as a militant group trying to undermine the social order, and the progress of the Gospel would have been greatly hindered.

B. SLAVES WITH BELIEVING MASTERS (1 TIM. 6:2). The

danger here is that a Christian slave might take advantage of his master because both are saved. "My master is my brother!" a slave might argue. "Since we are equal, he has no right to tell me what to do!" This attitude would create serious problems both in the homes and in the churches.

Paul gave three reasons why Christian slaves should show respect for their believing masters and not take advantage of them. The most obvious reason is: *Their masters are Christians* ("faithful"=believing). How can one believer take advantage of another believer? Second, *their masters are beloved*. Love does not rebel or look for opportunities to escape responsibility. Finally, *both master and servant benefit from obedience* ("partakers of the benefit" can apply to both of them). There is a mutual blessing when Christians serve each other in the will of God.

I recall counseling a young lady who resigned from a secular job to go to work in a Christian organization. She had been there about a month and was completely disillusioned.

"I thought it was going to be heaven on earth," she complained. "Instead, there are nothing but problems."

"Are you working just as hard for your Christian boss as you did for your other boss?" I asked. The look on her face gave me the answer. "Try working harder," I advised, "and show him real respect. Just because all of you in the office are saved doesn't mean you can do less than your best." She took my advice and her problems cleared up.

2. False teachers (1 Tim. 6:3-10)

Paul had opened this letter with warnings about false teachers (1:3ff), and had even refuted some of their dangerous teachings (4:1ff). The spiritual leaders in the local church must constantly oversee what is being taught, because it is easy for false doctrines to slip in (Acts 20:28-32). A pastor I know discovered a Sunday School teacher who was sharing his "visions" instead of teaching God's Word!

A. THE MARKS OF THESE FALSE TEACHERS (1 TIM. 6:3-5A). The first mark is that they refused to adhere to "the sound instruction of our Lord Jesus Christ and to godly teaching" (6:3, NIV). This teaching is godly and it promotes godliness. Isaiah's first test of any teacher was, "To the law and to the testimony: If they speak not according to this word, it is because there is no light in them" (Isa. 8:20). It is important that a church "hold fast the form of sound [healthy] words" (2 Tim. 1:13).

A second mark is the teacher's own attitude. Instead of being humble, a false teacher is proud; yet he has nothing to be proud about because he does not know anything (1 Tim. 6:4, also 1:7).

A believer who understands the Word will have a burning heart, not a big head (Luke 24:32; and see Dan. 9:1-20). This "conceited attitude" causes a teacher to argue about minor matters concerning "words" (1 Tim. 6:3). Instead of feeding on the "wholesome words of . . . Christ," you might say he gets sick about questions. The word "doting" (6:4) means "filled with a morbid desire, sick." The result of such unspiritual teaching is "envy, quarreling, malicious talk, evil suspicions, and constant friction" (6:4b-5a, NIV).

The tragedy of all this is that the people are "robbed of the truth" (6:5, NIV) while they think they are discovering the truth! They think that the weekly arguments in their meetings, during which they exchange their ignorance, are a means of growing in grace; when the result is a *loss* of character, not an improvement.

B. The motive for their teaching (1 Tim. 6:5b-10).
These false teachers supposed "that godliness is a way
of financial gain" (literal translation). "Godliness" here
(6:5) means "the profession of Christian faith" and not
true holy living in the power of the Spirit. They used
their religious profession as a means to make money.
What they did was not a true ministry; it was just a
religious business.

Paul was always careful not to use his calling and
ministry as a means of making money. In fact, he once
refused support from the Corinthian church, so that no
one could accuse him of greed (1 Cor. 9:15-19). He
never used his preaching as "a cloak of covetousness"
(1 Thes. 2:5). What a tragedy it is today to see the
religious racketeers who prey upon gullible people,
promising them help while taking away their money.

To warn Timothy—and us—about the dangers of
covetousness, Paul shared four facts:

1. Wealth does not bring contentment (1 Tim. 6:6).
The word "contentment" means "an inner sufficiency
that keeps us at peace in spite of outward circumstances." Paul used this same word later. "For I have
learned, in whatsoever state I am, therewith to be
content" (Phil. 4:11). True contentment comes from
godliness in the heart, not wealth in the hand. A
person who depends on material things for peace and
assurance will never be satisfied, for material things
have a way of losing their appeal. It is the wealthy
people, not the poor people, who go to psychiatrists
and who are more apt to try to commit suicide.

2. Wealth is not lasting (1 Tim. 6:7). I like to translate this verse: "We brought nothing into this world
because we can carry nothing out." (See Job 1:21.)
When someone's spirit leaves his body at death, it can
take nothing with it; because, when that person came

into the world at birth, he brought nothing with him. Whatever wealth we amass goes to the government, our heirs, and perhaps charity and the church. We always know the answer to the question, "How much did he leave?" *Everything!*

3. *Our basic needs are easily met (1 Tim. 6:8).* Food and "covering" (clothing and shelter) are basic needs; if we lose them, we lose the ability to secure other things. A miser without food would starve to death counting his money. I am reminded of the simple-living Quaker who was watching his new neighbor move in, with all of the furnishings and expensive "toys" that "successful people" collect. The Quaker finally went over to his new neighbor and said, "Neighbor, if ever thou dost need anything, come to see me, and I will tell thee how to get along without it." Henry David Thoreau reminded us that a man is wealthy in proportion to the number of things he can afford to do without.

The economic and energy crises that the world faces will probably be used by God to encourage people to simplify their lives. Too many of us know the "price of everything and the value of nothing." We are so glutted with luxuries that we have forgotten how to enjoy our necessities.

4. *The desire for wealth leads to sin (1 Tim. 6:9-10).* "They that *will be* rich . . ." is the accurate translation. It describes a person who has to have more and more material things in order to be happy and feel successful. But riches are a trap; they lead to bondage, not freedom. Instead of giving satisfaction, riches create additional lusts (desires); and these must be satisfied. Instead of providing help and health, an excess of material things hurts and wounds. The result Paul described very vividly: "Harmful desires . . . plunge

men into ruin and destruction" (6:9, NIV). It is the picture of a man drowning! He trusted his wealth and "sailed along," but a storm came and he sank.

It is a dangerous thing to use religion as a cover-up for acquiring wealth. God's laborer is certainly worthy of his hire (5:17-18), but his motive for laboring must not be money. That would make him a "hireling," and not a true shepherd (John 10:11-14). We should not ask, "How much will I get?" but rather "How much can I give?"

3. The pastor himself (1 Tim. 6:11-16, 20-21)

While caring for the needs of his people, Timothy needed to care for himself as well. "Take heed unto thyself" (4:16) was one of Paul's admonitions. The phrase "But thou" (6:11) indicates a contrast between Timothy and the false teachers. They were men of the world, but he was a "man of God." This special designation was also given to Moses (Deut. 33:1), Samuel (1 Sam. 9:6), Elijah (1 Kings 17:18), and David (Neh. 12:24); so Timothy was in good company.

Paul gave four admonitions to Timothy that, if obeyed, would assure him success in his ministry and a continued testimony as "a man of God":

A. FLEE (1 TIM. 6:11A). There are times when running away is a mark of cowardice. "Should such a man as I flee?" asked Nehemiah (Neh. 6:11). But there are other times when fleeing is a mark of wisdom and a means of victory. Joseph fled when he was tempted by his master's wife (Gen. 39:12), and David fled when King Saul tried to kill him (1 Sam. 19:10). The word "flee" that Paul used here did not refer to literal running, but to Timothy's *separating himself* from the sins of the false teachers. This echoes the admonition in 6:5: "From such withdraw thyself."

Not all unity is good, and not all division is bad. There are times when a servant of God should take a stand against false doctrine and godless practices, and separate himself from them. He must be sure, however, that he acts on the basis of biblical conviction and not because of a personal prejudice or a carnal party spirit.

B. FOLLOW (1 TIM. 6:11b). Separation without positive growth becomes isolation. We must cultivate these graces of the Spirit in our lives, or else we will be known only for what we oppose rather than for what we propose. "Righteousness" means "personal integrity."

"Godliness" means "practical piety." The first has to do with character, the second with conduct.

"Faith" might better be translated "faithfulness." It has well been said that the greatest ability is dependability.

"Love" is the *agape* love that sacrifices for the sake of others. It seeks to get, not to gain.

"Patience" carries the idea of "endurance," sticking to it when the going is tough. It is not a complacency that waits, but a courage that continues in hard places.

"Meekness" is not weakness, but instead is "power under control." Courageous endurance without meekness could make a person a tyrant. Perhaps "gentleness" expresses the meaning best.

C. FIGHT (1 TIM. 6:12-16). The verb means "Keep on fighting!" It is a word from which we get our English word *agonize*, and it applied both to athletes and to soldiers. It described a person straining and giving his best to win the prize or win the battle. Near the end of his own life, Paul wrote, "I have fought a good fight" (2 Tim. 4:7).

This "fight," however, is not between believers; it is between a person of God and the enemy around him.

He is fighting to defend the faith, that body of truth deposited with the church (see 6:20). Like Nehemiah of old, Christians today need to have a trowel in one hand for building, and a sword in the other hand for battling (Neh. 4:17). It is sad when some Christians spend so much time fighting the enemy that they have no time to do their work and build the church. On the other hand, if we do not stand guard and oppose the enemy, what we have built could be taken from us.

What is it that encourages us in the battle? We have "eternal life" and need to take hold of it and let it work in our experience. We have been called by God, and this assures us of victory. We have made our public profession of faith in Christ and others in the church stand with us.

Another encouragement in our battle is the witness of Jesus Christ our Saviour. He "witnessed a good confession" (6:13) before Pontius Pilate and did not relent before the enemy. He knew that God the Father was with Him and watching over Him, and that He would be raised from the dead. It is "God who makes all things alive" (literal translation), who is caring for us, so we need not fear. Timothy's natural timidity might want to make him shrink from the battle. But all he had to do was remember Jesus Christ and His bold confession, and this would encourage him.

Paul gave Timothy military orders: "I give thee charge" (verse 13, also 1:3). He was to guard the commandment and obey it. Why? Because one day the Commander would appear and he would have to report on his assignment! The only way he could be ready would be to obey orders "without spot or blame" (6:14, NIV).

The Greek word translated "appearing" (6:14) gives

us our English word *epiphany* which means "a glorious manifestation." In Paul's day, the word was used in the myths to describe the appearing of a god, especially to deliver someone from trouble. Paul used it of the first coming of Jesus Christ (2 Tim. 1:10), and of His return (2 Tim. 4:1, 8). We do not know when Christ will come again, but it will be "in His own time" (1 Tim. 6:15, NIV) and He knows the schedule. Our task is to be faithful every day and abide in Him (1 John 2:28).

The subject of 1 Timothy 6:16 is God, the God and Father of our Lord Jesus Christ. He is the *only* Ruler, though others may take the title. "Potentate" (6:15) comes from a word that means "power." The kings and rulers of the earth may think they have power and authority, but God is Sovereign over all (see Ps. 2).

"King of kings, and Lord of lords" (1 Tim. 6:15) makes us think of Jesus Christ (Rev. 17:14; 19:16); but here the title is applied to God the Father. Jesus Christ, of course, reveals the Father to us; so He can justly claim this title.

"Immortality" (1 Tim. 6:16) means "not subject to death." Man is subject to death, but God is not. Only God has immortality as an essential and inherent part of His being. He is "immortal, invisible, the only wise God" (1:17). Because God is not subject to death, He is Life and the Giver of life. He is incorruptible and not subject to decay or change. In this life, believers are in mortal bodies; but when Jesus Christ returns, we shall share His immortality (1 Cor. 15:50-58).

Keep in mind that Paul explained all these truths about God in order to encourage Timothy to "fight the good fight of faith" and not give up. We need not fear life, because God is the Ruler of all; and we need not fear death, because He shares immortality with us.

Timothy lived in the godless city of Ephesus, but

God dwells in glorious light. "And the sight of the glory of the Lord was like devouring fire" (Ex. 24:17). "Who coverest Thyself with light as with a garment" (Ps. 104:2). John's description of heaven emphasized the glory of God that gives light to the city (Rev. 21:11, 23-24; 22:5). Of course, light is a symbol of holiness (1 John 1:5-7). God dwells apart from sin, and God is glorious in His holiness.

It is impossible for a sinful human to approach the holy God. It is only through Jesus Christ that we can be accepted into His presence. Jacob saw God in one of His Old Testament appearances on earth (Gen. 32:30); and God allowed Moses to see some of His glory (Ex. 33:18-23). "No man hath seen God at any time" (John 1:18) refers to seeing God *in His essence*, His spiritual nature. We can only see manifestations of this essence, as in the person of Jesus Christ.

Why did Paul write so much about the person and glory of God? Probably as a warning against the "emperor cult" that existed in the Roman Empire. It was customary to acknowledge regularly, "Caesar is Lord!" Of course, Christians would say "Jesus Christ is Lord!" Only God has "honor and power everlasting" (1 Tim. 6:16b). If Timothy was going to fight the good fight of faith, he had to decide that Jesus Christ *alone* was worthy of worship and complete devotion.

D. BE FAITHFUL (1 TIM. 6:20-21). God had committed the truth to Paul (1:11), and Paul had committed it to Timothy. It was Timothy's responsibility to guard the deposit and then pass it along to others who would, in turn, continue to pass it on (2 Tim. 2:2). This is God's way of protecting the truth and spreading it around the world. We are stewards of the doctrines of the faith, and God expects us to be faithful in sharing His Good News.

The word "science" (1 Tim. 6:20) does not refer to the kind of technology we know today by that name. "*Knowledge* falsely so called" is a better translation. Paul referred here to the teachings of a heretical group called "Gnostics" who claimed to have "special spiritual knowledge." (The Greek word for "knowledge" is *gnosis*, pronounced NO-sis. An "agnostic" is one who does not know. A Gnostic is one who claimed to know a great deal.)

There is no need to go into detail here about the heretical ideas of the Gnostics. Paul's letter to the Colossians was written to counteract them. They claimed to have "special spiritual knowledge" from visions and other experiences. They also claimed to find "hidden truths" in the Old Testament Scriptures, especially the genealogies. They considered matter to be evil, and they taught that a series of "emanations" connected God with man. Jesus Christ, they said, was only the greatest of these emanations.

The Gnostics actually had a doctrine that was a strange mixture of Christianity, Oriental mysticism, Greek philosophy, and Jewish legalism. Like many of the Eastern cults we see today, it offered "something for everybody." But Paul summarized all that they taught in one devastating phrase: "profane and vain babblings." Phillips translates it "the godless mixture of contradictory notions."

Why should Timothy avoid these teachings? Because some who got involved in them "wandered from the faith" (6:21, NIV). Not only will wrong motives (a desire for money) cause a person to wander from the faith (6:10), but so will wrong teachings. These lies work their way into a person's mind and heart gradually, and before he realizes it, he is wandering off the path of truth.

4. The rich (1 Tim. 6:17-19)

Paul had already written about the danger of the love of money, but he added a special "charge" for Timothy to give to the rich. We may not think that this charge applies to us, but it does. After all, our standard of living today would certainly make us "rich" in the eyes of Timothy's congregation!

A. BE HUMBLE (1 TIM. 6:17a). If wealth makes a person proud, then he understands neither himself nor his wealth. "But thou shalt remember the Lord thy God; for it is He that giveth thee power to get wealth" (Deut. 8:18). We are not owners; we are stewards. If we have wealth, it is by the goodness of God and not because of any special merits on our part. The possessing of material wealth ought to humble a person and cause him to glorify God, not himself.

It is possible to be "rich in the world [age]" (1 Tim. 6:17) and be poor in the next. It is also possible to be poor in this world and rich in the next. Jesus talked about both (Luke 16:19-31). But a believer can be rich in this world and also rich in the next, if he uses what he has to honor God (Matt. 6:19-34). In fact, a person who is poor in this world can use even his limited means to glorify God, and discover great reward in the next world.

B. TRUST GOD, NOT WEALTH (1 TIM. 6:17b). The rich farmer in our Lord's parable (Luke 12:13-21) thought that his wealth meant security, when really it was an evidence of insecurity. He was not really trusting God. Riches are uncertain, not only in their value (which changes constantly), but also in their durability. Thieves can steal wealth, investments can drop in value, and the ravages of time can ruin houses and cars. If God gives us wealth, we should trust Him, the Giver, and not the gifts.

C. Enjoy what God gives you (1 Tim. 6:17c). Yes, the word "enjoy" is in the Bible! In fact, one of the recurring themes in Ecclesiastes is, "Enjoy the blessings of life now, because life will end one day" (2:24; 3:12-15, 22; 5:18-20; 9:7-10; 11:9-10). This is not sinful "hedonism," living for the pleasures of life. It is simply enjoying all that God gives us for His glory.

D. Employ what God gives you (1 Tim. 6:18-19). We should use our wealth to do good to others; we should share; we should put our money to work. When we do, we enrich ourselves spiritually, and we make investments for the future (see Luke 16:1-13). "That they may lay hold on eternal life" (1 Tim. 6:19) does not suggest that these people are not saved. "That they may lay hold on the life that is real" would express it perfectly. Riches can lure a person into a make-believe world of shallow pleasure. But riches *plus God's will* can introduce a person to life that is real and ministry that is lasting.

Paul's final sentence was not for Timothy alone, because the pronoun is plural: "Grace be with all of you." Paul had the entire church in mind when he wrote this letter, and certainly all of the elders, and not just Timothy. As leader of the church, Timothy needed to heed the word of the apostle; but all of his church members had a responsibility to hear and obey as well.

And so do we today.

A suggested outline of Titus

Key idea: Christians should maintain good
           works (3:8).

I. *CHURCH ORGANIZATION*—chapter 1
    1. Preach God's Word (1:1-4)
    2. Ordain qualified leaders (1:5-9)
    3. Silence false teachers (1:10-16)
II. *CHRISTIAN OBLIGATION*—chapters 2—3
    1. Older saints (2:1-4a)
    2. Young men and women (2:4b-8)
    3. Christian slaves (2:9-15)
    4. Christians as citizens (3:1-8)
    5. Problem people (3:9-11)
    6. Conclusion (3:12-15)

7
Our Man in Crete

Titus 1

While Timothy was laboring in metropolitan Ephesus, Titus had his hands full on the island of Crete. Titus was a Greek believer (Gal. 2:3) who had served Paul well on special assignments to the church in Corinth (2 Cor. 7:13-14; 8:6, 16, 23; 12:18). Apparently Titus had been won to Christ through Paul's personal ministry (Titus 1:4) as Timothy had been (1 Tim. 1:2). "As for Titus," Paul wrote, "He is my partner and fellow worker among you" (2 Cor. 8:23, NIV).

But the people on the island of Crete were not the easiest to work with, and Titus became somewhat discouraged. Like Timothy, he was probably a young man. But unlike Timothy, he was not given to timidity and physical ailments. Paul had been with Titus on Crete and had left him there to correct the things that were wrong. Since Jews from Crete were present at Pentecost (Acts 2:11), it is possible that they had carried the Gospel to their native land.

Titus had his share of problems! The churches needed qualified leaders, and the various groups in the churches needed shepherding. One group of false teachers was trying to mix Jewish law with the Gospel of grace (Titus 1:10, 14), while some of the Gentile believers were abusing the message of grace and turning it into license (2:11-15). By nature, the people of Crete were not easy to work with (1:12-13), and Titus needed extraordinary patience and love. It would have been easy for Titus to have "heard God's call to go elsewhere," but he stuck it out and finished his work.

As you read and study this letter, you will discover that it is a condensed version of Paul's first letter to Timothy. In this first chapter, Paul reminded Titus of three responsibilities he had to fulfill:

1. Preach God's Word (Titus 1:1-4)

In this rather lengthy greeting, Paul emphasized the importance of the Word of God. Four times he used the Greek preposition *kata*, the root meaning of which is "down." But in this context, *kata* helps us see the relationship between the ministry and the Word of God. Consider the four phrases:

A. "ACCORDING TO THE FAITH OF GOD'S ELECT" (TITUS 1:1A). Paul's ministry was governed by the Word of God. He was "a slave of God" (the only place Paul used this phrase) and "a messenger sent on a special commission" by Jesus Christ. But the purpose of his ministry was to share the faith, that body of truth contained in the Word of God. "God's elect" are those who have trusted Jesus Christ as their Saviour (1 Peter 1:1-5; Eph. 1:4).

B. "THE TRUTH WHICH IS AFTER [ACCORDING TO] GODLINESS" (TITUS 1:1B). "Godliness" is an important concept in this letter, just as it was in 1 Timothy, even though the actual word is used only once. But the repetition of "good works" emphasizes the point (Titus

1:16; 2:7, 14; 3:1, 5, 8, 14). The truth of the Gospel changes a life from ungodliness (2:12) to holy living. Sad to say, there were people in the churches on Crete, like some church members today, who professed to be saved, but whose lives denied their profession (1:12).

This faith in Jesus Christ not only saves us *today*, and makes our lives godly; but it also gives us hope for *the future* (1:2). We have assurance for the future because of God's promises, and God cannot lie. (See Num. 23:19.) We are born again "unto a living hope" (1 Peter 1:3, NIV), because we have trusted the living Christ. We believers have eternal life now (1 John 5:11-12; John 3:16); but when Jesus Christ returns, we will enjoy eternal life in an even greater way.

C. "ACCORDING TO THE COMMANDMENT OF GOD" (TITUS 1:3). God reveals His message through preaching. This does not mean the act of proclaiming the Word, but rather the *content* of the message. "It pleased God by the foolishness of preaching [the message of the Cross] to save them that believe" (1 Cor. 1:21). This Word of the Gospel was committed to Paul (see 1 Tim. 1:11), and he had committed it to Titus. This ministry was according to the commandment of God and was not given by men (Gal. 1:10-12).

As in 1 Timothy, the title "Saviour" is often repeated in Titus (1:3-4; 2:10, 13; 3:4, 6). The God-given written Word reveals the Saviour, because a Saviour is what sinners need. God's grace brings salvation, not condemnation (2:11). Jesus could have come to earth as a Judge, but He chose to come as a Saviour (Luke 2:10-11).

D. "AFTER THE COMMON FAITH" (TITUS 1:4). The word "common" means "to have in common." This faith is the possession of all of God's people and not just a selected few. Christians in different denominational groups may wear different labels, but all who possess the same saving faith share "the common salvation" (Jude 3). There was a definite body of truth deposited in the church, "the faith that was once for all entrusted to the saints" (Jude 3, NIV). Any departure from this "common faith" is false teaching and must not be tolerated in the church.

As you review these four statements, you can see that Paul related everything in his ministry to the Word of God. His calling and his preaching depended on faith in Christ. He wanted Titus to grasp this fact and to make the Word of God a priority in his ministry. Throughout all three of the Pastoral Epistles there is an emphasis on teaching the Word of God. Local churches ought to be "Bible institutes" where the Word of God is taught systematically and in a practical way.

2. Ordain qualified leaders (Titus 1:5-9)

One reason Paul had left Titus on the island of Crete was that he might organize the local assemblies and "set in order" the things that were lacking. That phrase is a medical term; it was applied to the setting of a crooked limb. Titus was not the spiritual dictator of the island, but he was Paul's official apostolic representative with authority to work. It had been Paul's policy to ordain elders in the churches he had established (Acts 14:23), but he had not been able to stay in Crete long enough to accomplish this task.

Several of the qualifications listed here (Titus 1:6-8) have already been discussed in our study of 1 Timothy 3:2-3: "blameless, the husband of one wife . . . not given to wine, no striker [not violent], not given to filthy lucre . . . a lover of hospitality . . . sober." The fact that these standards applied to Christians on the island of Crete as well as to those in the city of Ephesus proves that God's measure for leaders does not fluctuate. A big city church and a small town church both need godly men in places of leadership.

Now, consider nine additional qualifications:

A. "HAVING FAITHFUL CHILDREN" (TITUS 1:6b). "Faithful" means "believing." The bishop's children should be Christians. After all, if a servant of God cannot win his own children to Christ, what success can he expect with outsiders? This is the same principle Paul emphasized to Timothy (1 Tim. 3:5)—Christian living and Christian service must begin at home. The children in an elder's home must not only be saved, but must be good examples of obedience and dedication. To be accused of "riot" [wild living] or disobedience ["unruly," unable to be ruled] would disqualify their father from the eldership. This applies, of course, to children still at home, under the authority of their father.

Too often, new Christians feel a call to the ministry and want to be ordained before they have had a chance to establish their families in the faith. If the children are small, the problem is not too great; but mature children go through a tremendous shock when all of a sudden their household becomes "religious"! A wise father first wins his own family to Christ and gives them a chance to grow before he pulls up stakes and moves to Bible school. We would have fewer casualties in the ministry if this policy were followed more often.

B. "THE STEWARD OF GOD" (TITUS 1:7a). A steward does not own but manages all that his master puts into his hands. Perhaps the most famous steward in the Bible is Joseph, who had complete control over all of Potiphar's business (Gen. 39:1-9). The most important characteristic of a steward is *faithfulness* (1 Cor. 4:1-2; Matt. 25:21). He must use what his master gives him for the good and glory of his master, and not for himself personally (see Luke 16:1-13).

The elder must never say, "This is mine!" All that he has comes from God (John 3:27) and must be used for God. His time, possessions, ambitions, and talents are all loaned to him by the Lord; and he must be faithful to use them to honor God and build the church. Of course, *all* Christians ought to be faithful stewards, and not the pastors only!

C. "NOT SELF-WILLED" (TITUS 1:7b). "Not overbearing" (NIV), always pushing to have his own way. While church members ought to respect and follow the leadership of the elders, they should be certain that it is leadership and not dictatorship. A self-willed pastor is arrogant, will not take his people's suggestions and criticisms, and makes sure he always gets his own way.

D. "NOT SOON ANGRY" (TITUS 1:7c). He must not have a quick temper. There is a righteous anger against sin (Eph. 4:26), but most of our anger is unrighteous and directed against people. Of itself, temper is a good thing. A righteous man ought to get angry when wrongs are done. Someone has said, "Temper is such a wonderful thing that it's a shame to lose it." Wise counsel, indeed.

E. "A LOVER OF GOOD MEN" (TITUS 1:8a). "One who loves what is good" (NIV) is an alternate translation, and this would include good men. But it also includes good books, good music, good causes, and many other good things. A man is a good man because he has a good heart and surrounds himself with good things. It is difficult to believe that a dedicated servant of God would deliberately associate with things that are bad for him and his family.

F. "JUST" (TITUS 1:8B). "Upright" is a good translation. He should be a man of integrity who sticks by his word and who practices what he preaches. His conduct is righteous.

G. "HOLY" (TITUS 1:8C). "Unstained" gives the idea. "Be ye holy, for I am holy" (1 Peter 1:16). The root meaning of "holy" is "different." Christians are different from lost sinners, because Christians are new creations by the grace of God (2 Cor. 5:17).

H. "TEMPERATE" (TITUS 1:8D). "Self-controlled" is the meaning, and it applies to a man's appetites and actions. "Disciplined" is a synonym. A pastor must discipline his time so that he gets his work done. He must discipline his desires, especially when well-meaning members try to stuff him with coffee and cake! He must keep his mind and body under control, as he yields to the Holy Spirit (Gal. 5:23, where "temperance" means "self-control").

I. "HOLDING FAST THE FAITHFUL WORD" (TITUS 1:9). The word "faithful" was a favorite with Paul (see 1 Tim. 1:15; 4:9; 2 Tim. 2:11; Titus 3:8). God's Word is trustworthy, because God cannot lie (Titus 1:2). Because the Word is faithful, those who teach and preach the Word should be faithful. Again, Paul used the phrase "sound doctrine" which we have already met in 1 Timothy (1:10). It means "healthy doctrine" that promotes spiritual growth.

So the elders have a twofold ministry of the Word: (1) building up the church with "healthy" doctrine, and (2) refuting the false teachers who spread unhealthy doctrine. The naive church member who says, "We don't want doctrine! Just give us helpful devotional thoughts!" does not know what he is saying. Apart from truth (and this means Bible doctrine) there can be no spiritual help or health.

The mentioning of those who oppose true doctrine led Paul to give the third responsibility that Titus was to fulfill.

3. Silence false teachers (Titus 1:10-16)

It did not take long for false teachers to arise in the early church. Wherever God sows the truth, Satan quickly shows up to sow lies. Titus faced an enemy similar to that described in 1 Timothy—a mixture of Jewish legalism, man-made traditions, and mysticism. Paul gave three facts about these false teachers.

A. WHAT THEY WERE PERSONALLY. Paul had nothing good to say about them! They would not submit to God's Word or to the authority of God's servant, for they were *unruly*. "Rebellious" would be a good translation. Beware of teachers who will not put themselves under authority.

They were *vain talkers*. What they said impressed people, but it had no content or substance. When you "boiled it down," it was just so much hot air. Furthermore, they excelled in *talking*, not in *doing*. They could tell others what to do, but they did not do it themselves. Note especially Titus 1:16.

The great tragedy was that they *deceived* people by their false doctrines. They claimed to be teaching truth, but they were peddlers of error. Because they themselves were deceived by Satan, they deceived others, "teaching things they ought not to teach" (1:11, NIV).

They were *carnal* and *worldly:* "liars, evil brutes, lazy gluttons" (1:12, NIV). What an indictment! Instead of living for the beautiful things of the spiritual life, they lived for their own appetites. Paul's adjectives are arresting. These men were not just "beasts," but "*evil* beasts"; they were not just "gluttons," but "*lazy* gluttons." They were celebrities, not servants. They "lived it up" at the expense of their followers, and (true to human nature), *their followers loved it!*

Paul summed up their character in verse 16. They were "abominable," which means "detestable, disgusting." Christians with good spiritual sense would be completely disgusted with the character and conduct of these teachers, and would never follow them. "Disobedient" means "they cannot and will not be persuaded." Their minds have been made up and they will not face the truth. "Reprobate" literally means "not able to pass the test." God does not use them because they have been proved unfit. This same Greek word is translated "castaway" in 1 Corinthians 9:27. There it is in an athletic context and means "disqualified."

Having described what these teachers were, Paul then shared a second fact.

B. WHAT THEY DID. The picture was clear: These false teachers told lies from house to house and thus upset the faith of the people. Whole families were affected by their unhealthy doctrines. For one thing, they were teaching Jewish legalism ("they of the circumcision," Titus 1:10 and see 3:9) which Paul rejected. They were also teaching "Jewish fables" (1:14), which probably described their fanciful interpretations of the genealogies in the Old Testament (1 Tim. 1:4).

It never ceases to amaze me what some people get out of the Scriptures! I was once on a telephone talk program on a Chicago radio station, discussing Bible prophecy. A man phoned in and tried to take over the program by proclaiming his strange interpretations of Daniel's prophecies. He rejected the clear explanation given in the Bible and was very upset with me when I refused to agree with his fanciful ideas.

Dr. David Cooper used to say, "When the plain sense of Scripture makes good sense, seek no other sense." There is no need to find "deeper meanings" to the plain teachings of the Word of God. Such an approach to the Bible enables a "student" to find anything he is looking for!

Since the early church assemblies usually met in private homes, it is easy to understand how "whole houses" (Titus 1:11) could be upset by false teachers. People today who have Bible study classes in their homes must be careful lest visitors come in with strange doctrines. There are sects and cults that look for these classes and plant their agents just for the purpose of winning converts, so we must be careful.

C. WHY THEY DID IT. Their main motive was to make money: "for filthy lucre's sake" (1:11). They were not ministering to the church; they were using religion to fill their own pockets. This explains why Paul said that "not given to filthy lucre" was one requirement for an elder. A true servant of God does not minister for personal gain; he ministers to help others grow in the faith.

But behind this covetousness was another problem: Their minds and consciences had been defiled (1:15). This is what happens when a person lives a double life: Outwardly, he commands respect; but inwardly, he deteriorates. No one can serve two masters. These deceivers' love for money caused them to teach false doctrine and live false lives, and the result was a defiled conscience *that did not convict them*. This is one step closer to that "seared conscience" that Paul wrote about (1 Tim. 4:2).

Titus 1:15 is one of those verses that some ignorant people try to use to defend their ungodly practices.

"To the pure, all things are pure" is used to excuse all sorts of sin. I recall warning a teenager about the kind of literature he was reading, and his defense was, "Beauty is in the eye of the beholder. Your heart must be filthy if you see sin in what I'm reading. After all, 'To the pure, all things are pure.' "

To begin with, Paul was refuting the false teaching of these legalists with reference to *foods*. They were teaching that the Jewish dietary laws still applied to Christian believers (see 1 Tim. 4:3-5). If you ate forbidden food, you defiled yourself; but if you refused that food, you became holier.

"It is just the opposite," Paul argued. "These teachers have defiled minds and consciences. Therefore, when they look at these innocent foods, they see sin, because sin has defiled their vision. But those of us who have pure minds and consciences know that all foods are clean. It is not the foods which are defiling the teachers; it is the teachers who are defiling the foods!"

But this principle must not be applied to things that we know are evil. The difference, for example, between great art and pornography is more than "in the eye of the beholder." A great artist does not exploit the human body for base gain. For a believer to indulge in sinful erotic experiences, and claim that they were pure because his heart was pure, is to use the Word of God to excuse sin. The application Paul made was to foods, and we must be careful to keep it there.

Having shared these three facts about these false teachers, Paul added one further matter.

D. WHAT TITUS WAS TO DO. He was not to stand quietly by and let them take over! First, he was to "exhort and to convince" them by means of "sound doctrine" (Titus 1:9). The only weapon against Satan's lies is God's truth. "Thus saith the Lord!" is the end of every argument.

Titus was to stop their mouths (1:11) and prevent them from teaching and spreading false doctrines. He was to "rebuke them sharply" (1:13). Paul would give this same counsel to Timothy in his final letter: "Reprove, rebuke, exhort with all long-suffering and doctrine" (2 Tim. 4:2).

Paul's purpose, of course, was to convince these teachers and get them to be "sound in the faith" (Titus 1:13). But while he is doing this, he must protect the church from their false teachings. False doctrine is like yeast: It enters secretly, it grows quickly, and it permeates completely (Gal. 5:9). The best time to attack false doctrine is at the beginning, before it has a chance to spread.

The attitude of some church members is, "It makes no difference what you believe, just as long as you believe something." Paul would not agree with that foolish philosophy. It makes all the difference between life and death whether or not you believe the truth of the Word or believe lies. You can choose what you want to believe, but you cannot change the consequences.

"And ye shall know the truth," said Jesus Christ, "and the truth shall make you free" (John 8:32).

8
How to Have a Healthy Church

Titus 2—3

In contrast to the false teachers, Titus was to "speak the things which belong to healthy doctrine" (2:1, literal translation). What germs are to a physical body, false teaching is to a spiritual body, the church. In the verses that make up this section, you will find a beautiful blending of doctrinal teaching and practical admonition, for the two must go together. Paul discussed several different areas of ministry in the local church.

1. The older saints (Titus 2:1-4a)

How easy it would be for a younger man like Titus to misunderstand or even neglect the older members of his congregation.

"I want a church of young people!" a pastor once said to me, forgetting that one day he would be old himself. A church needs both the old and the young, and they should minister to one another. The grace of God enables us to bridge the generation gap in the church. One way to do this is for all members, young and old, to live up to the standards that God has set for our lives.

The older men were to be *sober*, which means "to be temperate in the use of wine." Old men with time on their hands could linger too long over the cup.

Grave means "dignified," but it does not suggest a solemn person who never laughs. There is a dignity to old age that produces respect, and this respect gives the older saint authority. How I thank God for the venerable saints who have assisted me in my own pastoral ministry! When they stood to speak, the whole church listened and took heed.

Temperate describes an attitude of mind that leads to prudence and self-control in life. It is the opposite of frivolity and carelessness that are based on ignorance. It is translated "sober" in Titus 1:8 and 2:4, 6, and 12, and "discreet" in 2:5. Seriousness of life and purpose are important in the Christian life, and especially to older saints who cannot afford to waste time, for their time is short.

Sound in faith, in love, in patience all go together. The older men should know what they believe, and their doctrinal convictions should accord with God's Word. For a knowledge of Bible doctrine is no substitute for the other necessary virtues, such as love for the brethren and patience in the trials of life. In fact, a right faith in God's Word should encourage a believer in love and endurance.

It is possible that the word "likewise" in verse 3 means that the older women were to have the same qualities as the older men, plus the additional ones listed. The deportment (behavior) of these older women must always reflect holiness. They must not be slanderers ("false accusers"—the Greek word is "devils" which means "slanderers"), picking up gossip and spreading it. They must also be temperate in their use of wine.

When it comes to the older women, Paul's emphasis is on *teaching:* "teachers of good things." Experienced, godly women are usually excellent teachers. The word "teach" in 2:4 is related to the word translated "temperate" in verse 2, and probably should be translated, "that they may train by making sober-minded." It is not only that the older women show the younger mothers how to keep house, but that they put within their hearts and minds the right spiritual and mental attitudes.

One of the strongest forces for spiritual ministry in the local church lies with the older believers. Those who are retired have time for service. It is good to see that many local churches have organized and mobilized these important people. In my own ministry, I have been greatly helped by senior saints who knew how to pray, teach the Word, visit, troubleshoot, and help build the church.

2. The younger saints (Titus 2:4b-8)

The godly older women have the responsibility of teaching the younger women how to be successful wives, mothers, and housekeepers; and the younger women have the responsibility of listening and obeying. The Christian home was a totally new thing, and young women saved out of paganism would have to get accustomed to a whole new set of priorities and privileges. Those who had unsaved husbands would need special encouragement.

The greatest priority in a home should be love. If a wife loved her husband and her children, she was well on the way to making the marriage and the home a success. In our Western society, a man and woman fall in love and then get married; but in the East, marriages were less romantic. Often the two got married and then had to learn to love each other. (Ephesians 5:18-33 is probably the best Scripture for a husband and wife who really want to love each other in the will of God.)

Surely a mother loves her children! Yes, this is a natural instinct; but this instinct needs to be controlled. I once heard a "modern mother" say, "I love my child too much to spank her." In reality, she had a selfish love for herself and did not really love the child. "He who spares the rod hates his son, but he who loves him is careful to discipline him" (Prov. 13:24, NIV). While it was usually the father who disciplined the children in Eastern homes, the mother could not escape being a part of the procedure, or else a child would run to its mother for protection.

"To be discreet" (Titus 2:5) is our familiar word "sober-minded" again ("temperate" in verse 2). Outlook determines outcome; and if a person is not thinking rightly, he will not act properly. A woman needs a correct and disciplined outlook on her ministry in the home. "Self-controlled" is the idea contained in this word. If parents do not discipline themselves, they can never discipline their children.

"Chaste" means "purity of mind and heart." A Christian wife is true to her husband in mind and heart as well as in action.

"Keepers at home" does not suggest that her home is a prison where she must be kept! "Caring for the home" is the idea. "Guide the house" Paul wrote (1 Tim. 5:14). The wise husband allows his wife to manage the affairs of the household, for this is her ministry.

"Good" (Titus 2:5) can be translated "kind." She

does not rule the household with an iron hand, but practices "the law of kindness" (Prov. 31:26).

While the wife is "busy at home" (NIV), it is the husband who is the leader in the home; so the wife must be obedient. But where there is love (Titus 2:4) there is little problem with obedience. And where the desire is to glorify God, there is no difficulty that cannot be worked out.

"That the Word of God be not blasphemed" is a good motive for cooperation and obedience at home. It is sad to see the way family problems, and even divorces, among Christians cause unsaved people to sneer at the Gospel and the Bible.

Titus was to let the older women minister to the younger women, lest he get himself in a difficult situation. But he was to be an example to the younger men with whom he would easily identify. Exhortation and example were to be his tools for building them up in the faith (2:6-7). He was to exhort them to be self-controlled, for there were many temptations to sin.

But Paul wrote more about Titus the *example* than he did about Titus the *exhorter!* A pastor preaches best by his life. He must constantly be a good example in all things. Whatever the pastor wants his church to be, he must first be himself. "For they say, and do not" was our Lord's indictment against the Pharisees (Matt. 23:3). This is hypocrisy.

The Greek word *tupos* ("pattern," Titus 2:7) gives us our English word "type." The word originally meant "an impression made by a die." Titus was so to live that his life would be like a "spiritual die" that would impress itself on others. This involved good works, sound doctrine, a seriousness of attitude, and sound speech that no one—not even the enemy—could condemn. Whether we like it or not, there are "contrary" people who are always looking for a fight. A pastor's speech should be such that he stands without rebuke.

It is not easy to pastor a church. You do not punch a clock; yet you are always on duty. You must be careful to practice what you preach; you must be the same man in and out of the pulpit. Hypocrisy in speech or conduct will ruin a man's ministry. No pastor is perfect, just as no church member is perfect; but he must strive to be the best example possible. A church will never rise any higher than its leadership.

3. Christian slaves (Titus 2:9-15)

Paul usually had a word concerning the slaves (see Eph. 6:5-9; 1 Tim. 6:1-2). We are glad for this word to Titus because Paul backed it up with one of the greatest statements about salvation found in the New Testament. Paul always linked doctrine and duty.

Paul warned these Christian slaves about three common sins they must avoid (Titus 2:9-10). First, *disobedience*. They were to obey their masters and seek to please them, which meant going the extra mile. It is possible to obey, but not "from the heart" (Eph. 6:6). It is possible to do a job grudgingly. Some unsaved masters would not be thoughtful and would overwork their slaves.

The second sin was *talking back* ("answering again," Titus 2:9). While a slave would not carry this too far (his master might severely discipline him), he could argue with his master since the master probably knew less about the job than the slave did. The slave could also "gripe" about his master to others on the job. This would certainly be a poor testimony for a Christian slave.

Christian slaves were also to avoid the sin of *stealing* ("purloining"). This was the sin Onesimus probably committed against Philemon (see Phile. 18). It would be easy for a slave to pilfer little items and sell them, and then report that they had been broken or lost.

There are no slaves in our society today, but there are employees. Christian workers must obey orders and not talk back. They must not steal from their employers. Millions of dollars are lost each year by employers whose workers steal from them, everything from paper clips and pencils to office machines and vehicles. "They owe it to me!" is no excuse. Neither is, "Well, I've earned it!"

Paul gave a good reason why Christian workers should be trustworthy ("showing all good fidelity"): This will "embellish with honor" the Word of God (Wuest's *Expanded Translation*). When we serve faithfully, we "beautify the Bible" and make the Christian message attractive to unbelievers. When Paul addressed the slaves in Timothy's church (1 Tim. 6:1), he used a negative motive: "that the name of God and His doctrine be not blasphemed." Both the positive motive—to make God's message attractive—and the negative motive—to keep God's teaching from being slandered—ought to control our lives.

Here (Titus 2:11) Paul expanded the meaning of "Saviour" (v. 10), by explaining what was involved in this salvation that we have through Jesus Christ. The emphasis is on *grace*—God's lavish favor on undeserving sinners. Paul pointed out three wonderful ministries of the grace of God (2:11-14):

A. GRACE REDEEMS US (TITUS 2:11, 14A). People could not save themselves. God's grace had to bring salvation to lost mankind. This salvation was not discovered by sinners; it appeared to them via the life, death, and resurrection of Jesus Christ. God in His grace sent His Son to redeem those in the bondage of sin. This salvation is for "all men" who receive it (see 1 Tim. 2:4-6). There is a universal need, and God provided a universal remedy for all who will believe.

Paul explained this salvation further (Titus 2:14). Christ "gave Himself for us," which means that He became our substitute. "Who His own self bare our sins in His own body on the tree" (1 Peter 2:24). The word "redeem" means "to set free by paying a price." We were all slaves of sin (Titus 3:3) and could not set ourselves free; but Jesus Christ gave Himself as the ransom for our sins. By His death, He met the just demands of God's holy law, so that God in His grace could forgive and free those who believe on Christ.

We have been redeemed "from all iniquity," which means that sin should no longer master our lives. (Remember that the context of this passage is Paul's counsel to *slaves*. They knew the meaning of "redeem.") "Iniquity" means "lawlessness." In our unsaved condition, we were rebels against God's law; but now all of that has been changed. This led Paul to the second ministry of the grace of God.

B. GRACE REFORMS US (TITUS 2:12, 14B). Salvation is not only a change in position (set free from the slavery of sin); but it is also a change in attitude, appetite, ambition, and action. The same grace that redeems us also reforms our lives and makes us godly. "Teaching" has the idea of "disciplining." We are disciplined by God's grace, trained to be the kind of people that glorify Him.

Godly living involves the negative and the positive. We deny "ungodliness [whatever is unlike God] and worldly lusts" (see 1 John 2:15-17). The verb means that we do it once and for all. It is a settled matter. Then, we work on the positive. "Soberly" is our familiar word for "self-control, prudence, restraint" (see

2:2). This emphasizes the believer's relationship to himself, while "righteously" deals with his relationships with other people. "Godly" speaks of his relationship to the Lord, though the two qualities must not be separated.

Christians live "in this present age" (NIV), but they do not live *like* it or *for* it. Christ has redeemed us from this evil age (Gal. 1:4), and we must not be conformed to it (Rom. 12:1-2). Neither should we walk according to its standards (Eph. 2:2). We have tasted the powers of "the coming age" (Heb. 6:5, NIV), and we should not desire to cultivate the present age with its shallowness and godlessness.

Grace reforms us because God purifies us and makes us His own special possession (Titus 2:14b). This process of purification is called "sanctification," and its goal is to make the believer more like Jesus Christ (Rom. 8:29). Sanctification is not only separation from sin, but it is also devotion to God (2 Cor. 6:14—7:1). "Peculiar" does not mean "odd" or "strange." It means "a special people for God's own possession" (see Deut. 14:2; 26:18).

C. GRACE REWARDS US (Titus 2:13). We are looking for Jesus Christ to return; this is our only hope and glory. This verse boldly affirms that Jesus Christ is God, for there is only one article in the Greek: "the great God and our Saviour." Paul did not go into detail about the events surrounding the return of Christ. Believers should always be expecting His return and live like those who will see Him face to face.

4. Christians as citizens (Titus 3:1-8)

Christians were often looked on with suspicion in the Roman Empire, because their conduct was so different and they met in private meetings for worship (see 1 Peter 2:11-25 and 3:13—4:5). It was important that they be good citizens without compromising the faith. Their pagan neighbors might disobey the law but Christians must submit to the authority of the state (see Rom. 13). "Ready to every good work" (Titus 3:1) means "cooperating in those matters that involve the whole community." Our heavenly citizenship (Phil. 3:20) does not absolve us from responsibilities as citizens on earth.

The believer should not have a bad attitude toward the government and show it by slanderous accusations and pugnacious actions. The word "gentle" (Titus 3:2) means "an attitude of moderation, a sweet reasonableness." The person with this quality does not insist on the letter of the law, but is willing to compromise where no moral issue is at stake. "Meekness" is that disposition that keeps one's power under control.

Again, Paul linked duty to doctrine. "Don't be too critical of your pagan neighbors," he wrote. "Just remember what you were before God saved you!" Verse 3 needs little explanation; we know what it means from our own experience.

What a difference "the kindness and love of God" (3:4) made! If you want a beautiful illustration of "the kindness of God," read 2 Samuel 9 and note David's treatment of Mephibosheth, a little lame prince. Because Mephibosheth was a part of Saul's family, he expected to be slain. But David, in kindness, spared him and treated him as one of his own sons, at the palace table.

Salvation came not only because of God's kindness and love, but also because of His mercy (Titus 3:5). We did not save ourselves; "He saved us." How did He do it? Through the miracle of the new birth, the work of the Holy Spirit of God. I do not think that "washing" here refers to baptism, because in New Testament times, people were baptized *after* they were saved, and not in order to be saved (see Acts 10:43-48). "Washing" here means "bathed all over." When a sinner trusts Christ, he is cleansed from all his sins, and he is made a "new person" by the indwelling Holy Spirit.

Paul related this same cleansing experience to the Word of God (Eph. 5:26). Salvation comes to a sinner when he trusts Christ, when the Spirit of God uses the Word of God to bring about the new birth. We are born of the *Spirit* (John 3:5-6, where "water" refers to physical birth, which Nicodemus had mentioned earlier, v. 4), and of the *Word* (1 Peter 1:23-25). "Which" in Titus 3:6 ought to be "whom," referring to the Holy Spirit who is given to us at conversion (Acts 2:38; Rom 8:9; 5:5).

Not only have we who are Christians been washed and made new in Christ, but we have also been *justified* (Titus 3:7). This wonderful doctrine is discussed in detail in Romans 3:21—8:39. Justification is the gracious act of God whereby He declares a believing sinner righteous because of the finished work of Christ on the Cross. God puts to our account the righteousness of His Son, so that we can be condemned no more. Not only does He forget our sins, but He forgets that we were even sinners!

What is the result of this kindness, love, mercy, and grace? Hope! We are heirs of God! This means that today we can draw on His riches; and when He comes, we will share His wealth and His kingdom forever. This hope ties in with Titus 2:13, "Looking for that blessed hope." But there is something more involved: We should live godly lives, and be "careful to maintain good works" (3:8). The only evidence the unsaved world has that we belong to God is our godly lives.

"Good works" do not necessarily mean religious works or church work. It is fine to work at church, sing in the choir, and hold an office; but it is also good to serve our unsaved neighbors, to be helpful in the community, and to have a reputation for assisting those in need. Baby-sitting to relieve a harrassed young mother is just as much a spiritual work as passing out a Gospel tract. The best way a local church has to witness to the lost is through the sacrificial service of its members.

5. Problem people (Titus 3:9-11)

We wish we did not have "problem people" in our churches; but wherever there are people, there can be problems. In this case, Paul warned Titus to avoid people who like to argue about the unimportant things of the faith. I recall being approached by a young man after a Bible lesson and getting involved with him in all sorts of hypothetical questions of doctrine. "Now, if this were true . . . if that were true . . ." was about all he could say. I was very inexperienced at the time; I should have ignored him in a gracious way. As it was, I missed the opportunity to talk with several sincere people who had personal problems and wanted help. I have learned that professed Christians who like to argue about the Bible are usually covering up some sin in their lives, are very insecure, and are usually unhappy at work or at home.

But there is another kind of problem person we should deal with: the "heretic." This word means "one who makes a choice, a person who causes divisions." This is a self-willed person who thinks he is right, and who goes from person to person in the church forcing people to make a choice. "Are you for *me* or for the pastor?" This is a work of the flesh (see Gal. 5:20). Such a person should be admonished at least twice, and then rejected.

How do we apply this in a local church? Let me suggest one way. If a church member goes about trying to get a following, and then gets angry and leaves the church, let him go. If he comes back (maybe the other churches don't want him either), and if he shows a repentant attitude, receive him back. If he repeats this behavior (and they usually do), receive him back the second time. But if he does it a third time, do not receive him back into the fellowship of the church (Titus 3:10). Why not? "Such a man is warped in character, keeps on sinning, and has condemned himself" (3:11, literal translation). If more churches would follow this principle, we would have fewer "church tramps" who cause problems in various churches.

6. Conclusion (Titus 3:12-15)

In the closing verses, Paul conveyed some personal information to Titus, and reminded him of the main theme of the letter: Insist that God's people "learn to devote themselves to doing what is good, in order that they may provide for daily necessities and not live unproductive lives" (3:14, NIV).

We know nothing about Artemas; Tychicus we have met in Acts 20:4. He was with Paul in his first Roman imprisonment, and carried the epistles from Paul to the Ephesians (Eph. 6:21), the Colossians (Col. 4:7-8), and to Philemon (cf. Col. 4:7-9 with Phile. 10). Either Artemas or Tychicus would replace Titus on Crete, and then Titus was to join Paul at Nicopolis.

It is possible that Zenas and Apollos (see Titus 3:13; Acts 18:24ff) carried this letter to Titus. Paul had sent them on a special mission and Titus was to aid them all he could.

Paul ended the letter to Titus with a variation of his usual benediction (see 2 Thes. 3:17-18): "Grace be with you all."

Grace—and good works! They go together!

A suggested outline of 2 Timothy

Theme: preparation for the ministry in the last days

Paul used four appeals to encourage Timothy:

I. *THE PASTORAL APPEAL*—chapter 1
    1. Courageous enthusiasm (1:1-7)
    2. Shameless suffering (1:8-12)
    3. Spiritual loyalty (1:13-18)

II. *THE PRACTICAL APPEAL*—chapter 2
    1. The steward (2:1-2)
    2. The soldier (2:3-4, 8-13)
    3. The athlete (2:5)
    4. The farmer (2:6-7)
    5. The workman (2:14-18)
    6. The vessel (2:19-22)
    7. The servant (2:23-26)

III. *THE PROPHETIC APPEAL*—chapter 3
    1. Turn away from the false (3:1-9)
    2. Follow those who are true (3:10-12)
    3. Continue in God's Word (3:13-17)

IV. *THE PERSONAL APPEAL*—chapter 4
    1. Preach the Word (4:1-4)
    2. Fulfill your ministry (4:5-8)
    3. Be diligent and faithful (4:9-22)

9
Christians
Courageous!

2 Timothy 1

When Paul wrote the letter we know as 2 Timothy, his situation had changed drastically. He was now a prisoner in Rome and was facing certain death (2 Tim. 4:6). For one reason or another, almost all of Paul's associates in the ministry were gone and only Luke was at the apostle's side to assist him (4:11). It was a dark hour indeed.

But Paul's great concern was not himself; it was Timothy and the success of the Gospel ministry. As in his first letter to Timothy, Paul encouraged his beloved colleague to be faithful. As we have learned, Timothy was timid, suffered from physical ailments, and was tempted to let other people take advantage of him and not assert his authority as a pastor.

Paul sent Tychicus to replace Timothy at Ephesus so that Timothy might join Paul at Rome (4:9, 12). God would soon move Paul off the scene, and Timothy would have to take Paul's place and continue to give spiritual leadership to the churches. It would not be an easy task, but Timothy could succeed with the Lord's help. In this first chapter, Paul gave Timothy three essentials that he must possess to have success in his ministry.

1. Courageous enthusiasm (2 Tim. 1:1-7)

The ministry of the Gospel is no place for a "timid soul" who lacks enthusiasm. In fact, courageous enthusiasm is essential for success in *any* kind of work. Paul compared this attitude to stirring up a fire into full flame (1:6). We must not hastily conclude that Timothy was backslidden, or that the spiritual fire had gone out of his life. Rather, Paul was encouraging his associate to keep the fire burning brightly so that it might generate spiritual power in his life. Paul gave Timothy four encouragements:

A. PAUL'S LOVE (2 TIM. 1:1-2). "Timothy, my dearly beloved son" is much stronger than "Timothy, my own son in the faith" (1 Tim. 1:2). It is not that Paul loved Timothy less when he wrote that first letter, but that Paul was now expressing it more. As Paul's life drew to a close, he realized in a deeper way how dear Timothy was to him.

Paul's own circumstances were difficult, and yet he was greatly encouraged. For one thing, he was Christ's ambassador ("apostle"); and he knew that his Master would care for him. Whatever happened to him was in the hands of God, so there was no need to fear. Furthermore, Paul had "the promise of life" in Jesus Christ, and Christ had defeated death (1:10). No wonder Paul was able to extend to Timothy "grace, mercy, and peace." (It is worth noting that Paul added "mercy" to his greetings when he wrote to the pastors—1 Timothy 1:2; 2 Timothy 1:2; Titus 1:4. Paul knew that pastors need mercy!)

B. PAUL'S PRAYERS (2 TIM. 1:3-4). What an encouragement to know that the great apostle was praying for him! Paul, who knew Timothy's weaknesses and problems, was able to pray definitely and with a real burden on his heart. His praying was not routine; it was done with compassion and concern. Knowing that he would soon die, Paul was anxious that Timothy join him at Rome for those last days of fellowship and ministry. This would bring joy to Paul's heart.

We must not assume that Paul tried to defend his evil actions when he was a Jewish rabbi by claiming he did it all with "a pure conscience." After all, he was guilty of causing terror among Christians, forcing people to blaspheme by denying Christ, and agreeing to the murder of Stephen! It is true that Paul thought he was serving God (see John 16:2), and that he was in spiritual ignorance (1 Tim. 1:13), but these facts cannot guarantee a pure conscience.

Paul had known God from his earliest years because he was "an Hebrew of the Hebrews" (Phil. 3:5). His ancestors had given him the orthodox Jewish faith. But when he met Jesus Christ, Paul realized that his Jewish faith was but preparation for the fulfillment Christ gave him in Christianity. He did not serve God with a pure conscience "from his forefathers," as the King James Version says. Rather, he heard about the true God from his forefathers; and *now* he was serving that God with a pure conscience. The fact that he had a pure conscience helped give power to his prayers.

C. PAUL'S CONFIDENCE IN TIMOTHY (2 TIM. 1:5). Paul did not think that Timothy's tears were evidence of failure or insincerity. Paul was sure that Timothy's faith was genuine, and that this faith would see him through in spite of the troubles he was facing. Apparently Lois, Timothy's grandmother, was the first one in the family won to Christ; then his mother, Eunice, was converted. Timothy's father was a Greek (Acts 16:1), so Eunice had not practiced the orthodox Jewish faith. However, Timothy's mother and grandmother had seen to it that he was taught the Scriptures (2 Tim. 3:15); and this was great preparation for the hearing of the Gospel. When Paul came to Lystra on his first missionary journey that was probably the occasion for Timothy's conversion. When Paul returned on his second journey, he enlisted Timothy into Christian service.

Paul had watched Timothy's life and service during those years they were together. He was certain that Timothy's faith was genuine. In fact, Timothy's heritage was a great one; for he was reared in a godly home, trained by a wonderful apostle, and given marvelous opportunities for serving the Lord.

D. God's gift to Timothy (2 Tim. 1:6-7). Paul reminded Timothy of the time God called him into service and the local church ordained him. Paul had laid his hands on Timothy (1 Tim. 4:14). Through Paul, God had imparted to Timothy the spiritual gift he needed for his ministry. The laying on of hands was a common practice in apostolic days (Acts 6:6; 13:3), but no believer today has the same authority and privileges that the apostles did. Today, when we lay hands on people for the ministry, it is a symbolic act and does not necessarily import any special spiritual gifts to them.

It is the Holy Spirit who enables us to serve God, and through Him we can overcome fear and weakness. The word "fear" in 2 Timothy 1:7 means "timidity, cowardice." The Holy Spirit gives us power for witness and for service (Acts 1:8). It is futile for us to try to serve God without the power of the Holy Spirit. Talent, training, and experience cannot take the place of the power of the Spirit.

The Holy Spirit also gives us love. If we have love for lost souls and for the people of God, we will be able to endure suffering and accomplish the work of God. Selfishness leads to fear; because if we are selfish, we are interested only in what we will get out of serving God, and we will be afraid of losing prestige, power, or money. True Christian love, energized by the Spirit (Rom. 5:5), enables us to sacrifice for others and not be afraid. The Spirit gives love (Gal. 5:22).

He is also the One who gives self-control ("a sound mind"). This word is related to the words *sober* and *sobriety* that we often meet in the pastoral letters (Titus 1:8; 2:2, 4, 6, 12; 1 Tim. 2:9, 15). "Self-discipline" is a better translation of "sound mind" (2 Tim. 1:7). It describes a person who is sensibly-minded and balanced, who has his life under control. The *Amplified Version* reads, ". . . calm and well-balanced mind and discipline and self-control."

Timothy did not need any new spiritual ingredients in his life; all he had to do was "stir up" what he already had. Paul had written in his first letter, "Neglect not the gift that is in thee" (1 Tim. 4:14). Now he added, "Stir up—stir into flame—the gift of God." The Holy Spirit does not leave us, no matter how much we fail (John 14:16); but He cannot fill us, empower us, and use us if we neglect our spiritual lives. It is possible to grieve the Spirit (Eph. 4:30) and quench the Spirit (1 Thes. 5:19).

Timothy had every reason to be encouraged and to have spiritual enthusiasm in his ministry. Paul loved him and prayed for him. His experiences in life had been preparation for his ministry, and Paul was confident of the genuineness of Timothy's faith. The Spirit within him would give all the power needed for ministry. What more could he want?

2. Shameless suffering (2 Tim. 1:8-12)

"Not ashamed" is a key idea in this chapter: Paul was not ashamed (v. 12); he admonished Timothy not to be ashamed (v. 8); and he reported that Onesiphorus was not ashamed of Paul's chain (v. 16).

Paul gave Timothy a twofold admonition:

A. BE NOT ASHAMED OF THE LORD'S TESTIMONY (2 TIM. 1:8-10). Timothy's natural timidity might make it easy for him to avoid circumstances that demanded witness and involved suffering. Once again, Paul gave his associate needed encouragement.

1. God gives us power (2 Tim. 1:8). By nature, none of us enjoys suffering. Even our Lord prayed, "Father, if Thou be willing, remove this cup from Me" (Luke 22:42); and Paul prayed three times for God to remove his painful thorn in the flesh (2 Cor. 12:7-8). But suffering is a part of a faithful Christian life. Christians should not suffer because they have done wrong (1 Peter 2:20; 3:17); rather, they sometimes suffer because they have done right and served God. When we suffer for doing good, then we are sharing Christ's sufferings (Phil. 3:10) and suffering on behalf of the whole church (Col. 1:24).

Years ago, I read about a Christian who was in prison because of his faith. He was to be burned at the stake, and he was certain he would never be able to endure the suffering. One night, he experimented with pain by putting his little finger into the candle flame. It hurt, and he immediately withdrew it. "I will disgrace my Lord," he said to himself. "I cannot bear the pain." But when the hour came for him to die, he praised God and gave a noble witness for Jesus Christ. God gave him the power *when he needed it*, and not before.

2. *God has called us by His grace (2 Tim. 1:9)*. We are part of a great eternal plan that God determined "before the world began." God knows the end from the beginning. He has purposes for His people to accomplish for His glory. Suffering is a part of His plan. Jesus Christ suffered in the will of God when He was here on earth, and all those who trust in Him will also suffer.

The emphasis in this verse is on *grace*. God saved us; we did not save ourselves (Eph. 2:8-9; Titus 3:5). He called us, not on the basis of our good works, but wholly on the basis of His grace. It is His purposes that we are to fulfill; and if these purposes include suffering, then we can accept it by faith and know that God's will is best. This is not fatalism. It is confidence in the wise and loving plan of our gracious heavenly Father.

All of this grace was given to us in Jesus Christ. We could not earn it; we did not merit it. This is the grace of God!

3. *Christ has defeated death (2 Tim. 1:10)*. When we are timid it is because we are afraid. Of what are we afraid? Suffering and possible death? Paul himself was facing death as he dictated this letter. But Jesus Christ has defeated our last enemy, death! By His own death and resurrection, Christ has "abolished death" (made it inoperative, taken out the sting). "O death, where is thy sting? O grave, where is thy victory?" (1 Cor. 15:55)

Christ was not only the Destroyer of death (see Heb. 2:14-15), but He was also the Revealer of life and immortality. In the Old Testament the doctrines of eternal life, death, resurrection, and the eternal state were in the shadows. Here and there you find glimpses of light; but for the most part, the picture is dark. But then Jesus Christ shone His light on death and the grave. Through the Gospel, He has given us assurance of eternal life, resurrection, and the hope of heaven.

Religious groups that teach "soul sleep" and other strange doctrines usually get their ideas from the Psalms and Ecclesiastes. Instead of allowing the clear light of the New Testament to shine on the Old, they look at the New through the shadows of the Old! If you turn your back on the light of the Gospel, you will only cast another shadow and make the scene darker.

"Immortality" (2 Tim. 1:10, KJV) means "incorruptibility," and refers to the resurrection body. The present body is corruptible; it decays and dies. But the glorified body we shall have when we see Christ will not be subject to decay or death (1 Cor. 15:49-58; Phil. 3:21). In fact, the heavenly inheritance that we share will be "incorruptible and undefiled, and [one] that fadeth not away" (1 Peter 1:4).

B. BE NOT ASHAMED OF THE LORD'S PRISONER (2 TIM. 1:11-12). Though a prisoner, Paul was still bearing witness for the Gospel of Jesus Christ. Sad to say, the people in Ephesus had deserted Paul in his time of need (v. 15). Many of them could have come to Rome to witness on Paul's behalf, but they did not. They were even ashamed to be identified with the apostle! It would have made Timothy's ministry in Ephesus (and in the surrounding cities; see 4:13) much easier if he had gone along with the crowd; but Paul admonished him to remain true. He gave two reasons why Timothy should not be ashamed of his association with Paul, the prisoner:

1. *Paul was called by God (2 Tim. 1:11).* Jesus Christ had met Paul on the Damascus Road (Acts 9) and had personally called him into the ministry. Paul was a *herald* ("preacher") of the Gospel. In ancient times, a "herald" was the official messenger of the king

or emperor, and his message was treated with great respect. The fact that professed believers in Asia were rejecting Paul did not change his calling or his message.

2. *Paul was not only a herald; he was also an apostle, "one sent with a commission."* Not every Christian was an apostle of Jesus Christ, for a person had to meet certain qualifications and be chosen by the Lord personally, or through His Spirit (see Acts 1:15-26; 1 Cor. 9:1; 2 Cor. 12:12). An apostle represented Jesus Christ. To reject an apostle was to reject the Lord.

3. *Paul was a teacher of the Gentiles.* This meant that he shepherded local churches. It was this word "Gentiles" that put him into prison in Rome the first time (Acts 22:21ff). The Gentile believers in Asia should have shown their appreciation of Paul by rallying to his support; for, after all, it was he who brought them the Good News of salvation. But instead they were ashamed of him and tried not to get involved.

4. *Paul was confident in Christ (2 Tim. 1:12).* Paul was not ashamed! Why? Because he knew that Christ was faithful and would keep him. Note his emphasis on the person of Christ: "I know *whom* I have believed." Salvation is not the result of believing certain doctrines, though doctrines are important. A sinner is saved because he believes in a person—Jesus Christ the Saviour. Paul had deposited his soul in the care and keeping of the Saviour, and Paul was sure that Jesus Christ would faithfully guard that deposit. What difference did it make to Paul what happened on any certain day? What really mattered is what would happen on "that day" when Jesus Christ rewards His servants (see 1:18 and 4:8).

In these difficult days, it is important that we stand true to Christ and be willing to suffer for Him and not be ashamed. We may not be put into a prison, as was Paul; but we might suffer in other ways: the loss of friends, being bypassed for a promotion, loss of customers, being snubbed by people, etc. It is also important that we stand by God's servants who are suffering for righteousness' sake.

3. Spiritual loyalty (2 Tim. 1:13-18)

Throughout the centuries God's work has been done by men and women who stood steadfast in their hours of trial. It would have been convenient for them to have compromised, but they stood firm. Paul was such a man, and he encouraged Timothy to follow his example.

A. BE LOYAL TO GOD'S WORD (2 TIM. 1:13-14). God had given the deposit of spiritual truth to Paul (1 Tim. 1:11), and he had given it to Timothy (6:20). It was now Timothy's solemn responsibility to "hold fast" (2 Tim. 1:13) and "guard" (1:14, NIV) the precious deposit of Christian truth, and to pass it along to others (2:2).

The word "form" (v. 13) means "a pattern, an architect's sketch." There was a definite outline of doctrine in the early church, a standard by which teaching was tested. If Timothy changed this outline, or abandoned it, then he would have nothing by which he could test other teachers and preachers. We today need to hold fast to what Paul taught, and for the same reason.

However, note that Timothy's orthodoxy was to be tempered with "faith and love." "Speaking the truth in love" (Eph. 4:15) is the divine pattern. How easy it is to become pugnacious in our desire to defend the faith, a witch hunter who creates problems.

It was the Holy Spirit who committed the truth to Timothy, and He would help him guard it. Apart from the ministry of the Spirit, we are in the dark when it comes to understanding the Word of God. It is He who must teach us (John 16:13) and enable us to guard the truth and share it with others.

From the beginning of human history, Satan has opposed God's Word. "Yea, hath God said?" was Satan's first word to mankind (Gen. 3:1), and he continues to ask that question. Throughout the history of the church, the Word of God has been attacked, often by people *within* the church; yet it still stands today. Why? Because dedicated men and women have (like Paul and Timothy) guarded the deposit and faithfully handed it to a new generation of Christians. When a church or any other Christian organization goes liberal, it usually starts with a weakening of their leaders' convictions about the Word of God.

B. BE LOYAL TO GOD'S SERVANT (2 TIM. 1:15-18). The province of Asia in that day comprised the Roman districts of Lydia, Mysia, Caria, and Phrygia. Paul was forbidden to minister in this area on his second missionary journey (Acts 16:6); but on his third journey, he stayed nearly three years in Ephesus, the capital of Asia, and evangelized the entire area (Acts 19; 20:31). The seven churches of Asia were all in this area (Rev. 1:4, 11).

We do not know who Phygelus and Hermogenes (2 Tim. 1:15) were. It is likely that they were leaders in the church who opposed Paul and would not come to his defense in Rome. You would think that the Asian believers would have stood by Paul; but, instead, they were ashamed of him and, at the same time (whether they knew it or not) ashamed of Christ. (See 4:16.)

It was certainly a dark hour for Paul. Demas had forsaken him (4:10). His other associates had been sent to distant places of ministry. False doctrines were spreading in the church (2:17-18). How Paul would have loved to have been free to preach the Word and defend the faith—but he was in a Roman prison. It was up to Timothy to get the job done.

But there was one man who dared to leave Ephesus and come to Rome to assist Paul—Onesiphorus. His name means "profit-bearing," and he certainly was a profitable friend to Paul. It is possible that he was a deacon in the church at Ephesus ("ministered" in 1:18 comes from the word that gives us "deacon"). During Paul's ministry at Ephesus, Onesiphorus was a faithful minister, along with his household. Since Timothy had pastored the Ephesian church, he would know this choice saint.

Let me add here that every pastor is thankful for those faithful members who assist him in the work of the Lord. My wife and I have found choice saints in each of the three churches we have served—people whose homes were open to us (and they didn't tell the whole church we were there!), whose hearts felt our burdens and needs, and whose prayers sustained us in difficult times. These believers minister behind the scenes, but the Lord will reward them openly "in that day" (1:18).

Onesiphorus traveled from Ephesus to Rome and diligently looked for Paul so he might minister to the prisoner's needs. It seemed difficult for him to find his former pastor (1:17). Perhaps some of the Roman Christians were still opposed to Paul as they had been during his first imprisonment (see Phil. 1:12-17). Perhaps the Roman officials were not cooperative, and did not want their choice prisoner to receive any help. In his first imprisonment, Paul was in his own house (Acts 28:30); but now he was in a Roman prison under careful guard.

But Onesiphorus persisted! He located Paul and risked his own life to stand with him and assist him. Some students believe that Onesiphorus was also arrested and possibly executed. They base this on the fact that Paul greeted the "household of Onesiphorus" in 4:19, but not the man himself. Also, Paul asked for *present* mercies for the household, but *future* mercies for Onesiphorus (1:16, 18).

But the problem is this: If Onesiphorus was dead, then Paul prayed for the dead (1:18); and we have no authorization in the Bible to pray for the dead.

We have no proof that Onesiphorus was dead when Paul wrote this letter. The fact that Paul asked God to bless the man's household, but that he did not mention the man, simply means that at the time Onesiphorus was not with his household. "When he *was* in Rome" (v. 17) suggests that, at that writing, Onesiphorus was not in Rome. Therefore, he was somewhere between Rome and Ephesus; so Paul prayed for him and his household. There was no need to greet Onesiphorus, for Paul had just spent much time with him; so Paul only greeted his household.

Onesiphorus was not ashamed of Paul's chain. The apostle was manacled to a Roman soldier 24 hours a day. Onesiphorus could have invented many excuses for staying in Ephesus. But instead he made the dangerous journey to Rome and ministered to Paul. "He often refreshed me" was Paul's description of this man's ministry. The Greek word means "to cool again." "Bracing me like fresh air" is the way the *Amplified Bible* translates it. How we thank God for Christians who are "a breath of fresh air" in our hours of trial!

Were it not for Paul's letter, we would never know that Onesiphorus had served Paul and the church. But the Lord knew, and the Lord will reward him "on that day."

The essentials for a successful ministry have not changed: courageous enthusiasm, shameless suffering, and spiritual loyalty.

10
Getting the Picture

2 Timothy 2

While attending a convention, I noticed a man wearing
two name badges. When I asked him why, he replied,
"Oh, I'm having an identity crisis!"

Paul did not want Timothy to have an identity crisis,
so he carefully explained what a pastor is and does. (Of
course, the same principles apply to all Christians.)
Paul presented seven pictures of the Christian
minister.

1. The steward (2 Tim. 2:1-2)

The ministry is not something we get for ourselves
and keep to ourselves. We are stewards of the spiritual
treasure God has given us. It is our responsibility to
guard the deposit and then invest it in the lives of
others. They, in turn, are to share the Word with the
next generation of believers.

It is important that we get our original treasure from
the Word of God, and not from the ideas and philos-
ophies of men. We do not test modern teachers by
their popularity, education, or skill. We test them by

the Word of God, and particularly the doctrines of grace as given by Paul. It is not we who examine Paul to see if he is right; it is Paul who examines us!

It takes strength to teach the Word of God. We must dig out of the rich mines of Scripture the "gold, silver, precious stones" that are hidden there (see 1 Cor. 3:10-23; Prov. 2:1-10; 3:13-15; 8:10-21). This strength can only come from God's grace. The secret of Paul's great ministry was the grace of God (1 Cor. 15:10).

The ability to study, understand, and teach the Word of God is a gift of God's grace. "Apt to teach" is one of God's requirements for the pastor (1 Tim. 3:2; 2 Tim. 2:24). Apt to teach implies apt to learn; so a steward must also be a diligent student of the Word of God.

2. The soldier (2 Tim. 2:3-4, 8-13)

Paul often used military illustrations in his letters. This is not surprising since he lived in a military state and often was in prison himself. He described in these verses the characteristics of a "good soldier of Jesus Christ."

A. HE ENDURES HARDNESS (2 TIM. 2:3). Many people have the idea that the ministry is a soft job. Preachers are often the butt of jokes that suggest that preachers are lazy and should be ashamed of accepting their salaries. But a dedicated Christian minister is in a battle that requires spiritual endurance. (See Eph. 6:10ff.)

B. HE AVOIDS WORLDLY ENTANGLEMENTS (2 TIM. 2:4). He is totally committed to his commanding officer, the one who enlisted him. In our case, this is Jesus Christ. I recall reading a story about a Civil War soldier who happened to be a watchmaker. One day the bugle sounded and the men were told to break camp.

"But I can't go now!" the soldier complained. "I have a dozen watches to repair!"

It is sometimes necessary for a pastor, or a pastor's wife, to be employed because their church is not yet able to support them. This is a sacrifice on their part and an investment in the work. But a pastor who is fully supported should not get involved in sidelines that divide his interest and weaken his ministry. I have met pastors who spend more time on their real estate ventures than on their churches. Our purpose is to please the Lord, not ourselves.

C. HE MAGNIFIES JESUS CHRIST (2 TIM. 2:8-9). "Remember Jesus Christ!" is the way this phrase should be translated. It sounds almost like a war cry, like "Remember the Alamo!" or "Remember Pearl Harbor!" Jesus is the Captain of our salvation (Heb. 2:10) and our purpose is to bring honor and glory to Him. What an encouragement Jesus Christ is to a suffering Christian soldier! For He died and rose again, proving that suffering leads to glory, and that seeming defeat leads to victory. Jesus was treated as an evildoer, and His soldiers will be treated the same way.

The best way to magnify Christ is through the ministry of the Word. Paul was bound, but God's Word cannot be bound. "His Word runneth very swiftly" (Ps. 147:15). "The Word of God grew and multiplied" (Acts 12:24).

D. HE THINKS OF THE WHOLE ARMY (2 TIM. 2:10). "The elect" are God's people, chosen by His grace and called by His Spirit (2 Thes. 2:13-14). Paul not only suffered for the Lord's sake, but he also suffered for the sake of the church. There were yet many people to reach with the Gospel, and Paul wanted to help reach them. A soldier who thinks only of himself is disloyal and undependable.

E. HE TRUSTS HIS COMMANDING OFFICER (2 TIM. 2:11-13). This "faithful saying" is probably part of an early statement of faith recited by believers. (For other "faithful sayings" in the pastoral letters, see 1 Tim. 1:15, 4:9, and Titus 3:8.) It is faith in Jesus Christ that gives us victory (1 John 5:4). We do not fear the enemies, for He has already conquered them. Through our identification with Christ in death, burial, and resurrection, we have won the victory (see Rom. 6).

What a pair of paradoxes! Death leads to life! Suffering leads to reigning in glory! We have nothing to fear! The important thing is that we not "disown" our Lord; for if we disown Him here, He will disown us before the Father (Matt. 10:33). In that great "roll call" in glory, when the "medals" are given out, we will lose our reward if we disown His name.

But Paul makes it clear (2 Tim. 2:13) that even our own doubt and unbelief cannot change Him: "He abideth faithful; He cannot deny Himself." We do not put faith in our faith, or in our feelings, because they will change and fail. We put our faith in Christ. The great missionary, J. Hudson Taylor, often said, "It is not by trying to be faithful, but in looking to the Faithful One, that we win the victory."

3. The athlete (2 Tim. 2:5)

Paul sometimes used athletic illustrations in his writings—wrestling, boxing, running, and exercising. The Greeks and the Romans were enthusiastic about sports, and the Olympic and Isthmian games were important events to them. Paul had already urged Timothy to exercise like an athlete (1 Tim. 4:7-8). Now Paul admonished him to obey the rules.

A person who strives as an athlete to win a game and get a crown must be careful to obey all the rules of the game. In the Greek games in particular, the judges were most careful about enforcing the rules. Each competitor had to be a citizen of his nation, with a good reputation. In his preparations for the event, he had to follow specific standards. If an athlete was found defective in any matter, he was disqualified from competing. If after he had competed and won, and was found to have broken some rule, then he lost his crown. Jim Thorpe, a great American athlete, lost his Olympic medals because he participated in sports in a way that broke an Olympic rule.

From the human point of view, Paul was a loser. There was nobody in the grandstands cheering him, for "all they which are in Asia" had turned away from him (1:15). He was in prison, suffering as an evildoer. Yet, *Paul was a winner!* He had kept the rules laid down in the Word of God, and one day he would get his reward from Jesus Christ. Paul was saying to young Timothy, "The important thing is that you obey the Word of God, no matter what people may say. You are not running the race to please people, or to get fame. You are running to please Jesus Christ."

4. The farmer (2 Tim. 2:6-7)

This is another favorite image found in Paul's letters. Paul once compared the local church to a cultivated field in which all the believers worked together (1 Cor. 3:5-9). Each Christian has his particular task to perform—plowing, sowing, watering, or harvesting—but it is God alone who gives the increase.

Several practical truths are found in this image of the farmer and field. For one thing, *a farmer has to work*. If you leave a field to itself, it will produce mostly weeds. Solomon had this truth in mind when he wrote about the field of the sluggard (Prov. 24:30-34). Real ministry is hard work, and a pastor (and church members) ought to work in their spiritual field as diligently as a farmer works in his field. Pastors do not punch clocks, but they ought to be up in the morning and at their work just as if God blew a whistle for them.

A farmer needs patience. "See how the farmer waits for the land to yield its valuable crop and how patient he is for the fall and spring rains" (James 5:7, NIV). A pastor friend of mine often reminds me, "The harvest is not the end of the meeting—it is the end of the age."

A farmer deserves his share of the harvest. "The hardworking farmer should be the first to receive a share of the crops" (2 Tim. 2:6, NIV). Paul is stating here that a faithful pastor ought to be supported by his church. The same idea is found in 1 Corinthians 9:7, where Paul used a soldier, a farmer, and a herdsman to prove his point: "The laborer is worthy of his reward" (1 Tim. 5:18). Paul deliberately gave up his right to financial support so that nobody could accuse him of using the Gospel for personal gain (1 Cor. 9:14ff). But this policy is not required for all of God's servants.

As a local church grows and progresses, the people ought to faithfully increase their support of their pastors and other staff members. "If we have sown spiritual seed among you, is it too much if we reap a material harvest from you?" (1 Cor. 9:11, NIV) It is sad to see the way some local churches waste money and fail to care for their own laborers. God will honor a church that honors His faithful servants.

Something else is true in this image of the farmer: The spiritual leaders who share the Word with the people are the first ones to enjoy its blessings. The preacher and the teacher always get more out of the sermon or lesson than do the hearers, because they put much more into it. They also get great joy out of seeing planted seeds bear fruit in the lives of others. Farming is hard work, and it can have many disappointments; but the rewards are worth it.

5. The workman (2 Tim. 2:14-18)

The word "study" (2:15) has nothing to do with books and teachers. It is the word "be diligent, be zealous." It is translated this way in 2 Timothy 4:9 and 21, and also in Titus 3:12. The emphasis in this paragraph is that the workman needs to be diligent in his labors so that he will not be ashamed when his work is inspected. "Rightly dividing" means "cutting straight" and can be applied to many different tasks: plowing a straight furrow, cutting a straight board, sewing a straight seam.

The pastor is a workman in the Word. The Word is a treasure that the steward must guard and invest. It is the soldier's sword and the farmer's seed. But it is also the workman's tool for building, measuring, and repairing God's people. The preacher and teacher who use the Word correctly will build their church the way God wants it to be built. But a sloppy worker will handle God's Word deceitfully in order to make it say what he wants it to say (2 Cor. 4:2). When God tests our ministries in His local churches, some of it, sad to say, will become ashes (1 Cor. 3:10ff).

An approved worker diligently studies the Word and seeks to apply it to his own life. An ashamed worker wastes his time with other "religious duties" and has little or nothing to give his class or congregation. An approved worker does not waste his time arguing about "words to no profit" (2 Tim. 2:14), because he knows that such arguing only undermines God's work. (See 1 Tim. 6:4 and Titus 3:9.)

An approved workman will shun "godless chatter"

(2 Tim. 2:16, NIV; and see 1 Tim. 6:20), because he knows it only leads to more ungodliness. I fear that some "sharing times" do more harm than good as well-meaning people exchange their spiritual ignorance.

An approved workman knows that false doctrine is dangerous, and he will oppose it. Paul compared it to gangrene (2 Tim. 2:17). Much as gangrene spreads, infects, and kills other tissue, so false doctrine spreads and infects the body of believers, the church. This infection must be exposed and removed. Only the "sound [healthy] doctrine" of the Word of God can keep a church healthy and growing.

Paul named two men who were false teachers, and he also identified their error. It is likely that the Hymenaeus named here (2 Tim. 2:17) is the same man named in 1 Timothy 1:20. We know nothing about his associate, Philetus. Both of them "wandered from the truth" by teaching that the resurrection had already taken place. Perhaps they taught that salvation is resurrection in a spiritual sense, so a believer must not expect a physical resurrection. But the denial of a physical resurrection is a serious thing (see 1 Cor. 15:12ff), for it involves the resurrection of Christ and the completion of God's plan of salvation for His people. No wonder these false teachers were able to "overthrow the faith of some" (2 Tim. 2:18). The resurrection is a foundational truth of the Gospel.

Each of us as God's workmen will be either *approved* or *ashamed*. The word "approved" means "one who has been tested and found acceptable." The word was used for testing and approving metals. Each trial that we go through forces us to study the Word to find God's will. As we rightly use the Word, we succeed in overcoming our trials, and we are approved by

God. Martin Luther once said that prayer, study, and suffering make a pastor; and this is true. We cannot be approved unless we are tested.

What does it mean to be "ashamed"? Certainly it means that such a workman's work is below standard and cannot be accepted. It means loss of reward. In fact, in Paul's day, a builder was fined if he failed to follow the specifications. When the Lord judges our works, it will be revealed whether we as workmen have handled the Word of God honestly and carefully. Some who are now first will end up last!

6. The vessel (2 Tim. 2:19-22)

In this illustration, Paul described a "great house," which is the professing church. The *foundation* of the house is safe and secure because God's seal is on it. (In the Bible, a seal is a mark of ownership and security. No one would dare break a Roman seal.) Paul quoted Moses: "The Lord knoweth them that are His" (Num. 16:5). This refers to the Godward aspect of the Christian life: God chose us who trust Him as His elect (see 2 Tim. 2:10).

But there is also a manward aspect of the Christian life; "Let everyone that nameth the name of Christ depart from iniquity" (2:19). This refers back to Numbers 16:26, where the Lord warned the people to get away from the tents of Korah and the rebels. In other words, those who are the elect of God prove it by living godly lives. We are chosen in Christ "that we should be holy and without blame" (Eph. 1:4).

This great house not only has a solid foundation that is sealed, but it also has vessels (utensils of various kinds) for performing household functions. Paul divides the utensils into two categories: those of honor (gold and silver), and those of dishonor (wood and clay). He is not distinguishing different kinds of Christians, but rather is making a difference between true teachers of the Word and the false teachers he described (2 Tim. 2:16-18). A faithful pastor is like a gold or silver vessel that brings honor to Jesus Christ. The head of a house displays his most costly and beautiful utensils and gets honor from them. I remember the first time I viewed the crown jewels of England in the Tower of London, along with the priceless table vessels and utensils. I was overwhelmed with their glory and beauty. That is the kind of beauty God gives to His servants who faithfully handle the Word of God.

False teachers are not valuable; they are like wood and clay. They are utensils to dishonor, no matter how popular they may be today. Wood and clay will not survive the test of fire. It is worth noting that the name "Timothy" comes from two Greek words which together mean "God-honoring." Paul was encouraging Timothy to live up to his name!

The important thing is that the honorable vessels not be contaminated by the dishonorable ones. The word "these" (2:21) refers to the vessels of dishonor (2:20). Paul is admonishing Timothy to separate himself from false teachers. If he does, then God will honor him, set him apart, and equip him for service. "Useful to the Master" (2:21, NIV)—what a tremendous honor that is! A useful human vessel of honor does not get involved in the popular things of the world, even the "religious world." He must remain holy, and this means he must be separated from everything that would defile him.

This includes the sins of the flesh as well (2:22). Paul used a similar admonition in 1 Timothy 6:11-12— "Flee . . . follow . . . fight." True Bible separation is balanced: we flee sin, but we follow after righteousness. If we are not balanced, then we will be isolated instead of separated. In fact, God's man Paul commands us to fellowship "with them that call on the Lord out of a pure heart" (2 Tim. 2:22). After all, this is the purpose of the ministry of the Word (1 Tim. 1:5). It is sad when true believers are isolated because of a false view of separation.

For God to be able to use us as vessels, we must be empty, clean, and available. He will take us and fill us, and use us for His glory. But if we are filled with sin or defiled by disobedience, He will first have to purge us; and that might not be an enjoyable experience. In the "great house" of the professing church, there are true believers and false, true teachers of the Word and false. We must exercise spiritual discernment and be careful that we are vessels sanctified unto honor.

7. The servant (2 Tim. 2:23-26)

"Servant" (2:24) is the Greek word *doulos* which means "slave." So Paul called himself "a slave of Jesus Christ" (Rom. 1:1; Phil. 1:1). A slave had no will of his own; he was totally under the command of his master. Once we Christians were the slaves of sin, but now we are the slaves of God (Rom. 6:16ff). Like the servant in Old Testament days, we say, "I love my master . . . I will not go out free" (Ex. 21:5).

God's slave does not have an easy time teaching the Word. Satan opposes him and tries to trap his listeners (2 Tim. 2:26). Too, some people are just naturally difficult to teach. They enjoy "foolish and stupid arguments" (2:23, NIV) and have no desire to feed on the nourishing Word of God. Until you have experienced it, you have no idea how difficult it is to impart spiritual truth to some people.

How easy it would be to ignore them! But then Satan

would get them. Paul admonished Timothy to avoid the arguments that create strifes, but not to ignore the people. He must not argue or fight. He must be patient and gentle, teaching the Word of God in meekness. It is not enough just to expose error and refute it; we must also teach positive truths and establish the saints in the faith.

A servant of God must instruct those who oppose him, for this is the only way he can rescue them from Satan's captivity. Satan is a liar (John 8:44). He captures people by his lying promises, as he did Eve. (See Gen. 3 and 2 Cor. 11:3.) A servant's purpose is not to win arguments but to win souls. He wants to see deceived persons brought to repentance ("I was wrong—I have changed my mind") and the acknowledging of the truth.

The word "recover" (2 Tim. 2:26) describes a man coming out of a drunken stupor. Satan makes people drunk with his lies, and the servant's task is to sober them up and rescue them. The last phrase in verse 26 can be interpreted three ways: (1) they are delivered from the snare of the devil who took them captive to do his will; (2) they are taken captive by God's servant to do God's will; (3) they are delivered out of the snare of the devil, who took them captive, to do God's will. I prefer the third interpretation.

As you survey these seven aspects of the work of the ministry, you can see how important and how demanding a work it is. The ministry is no place for a loafer, because it demands discipline and work. It is no place for a shirker, because there are enemies to fight and tasks to be completed.

Church members need to pray for their pastors, and encourage them in the work of the Lord. Church officers should faithfully do their work so that the pastors can devote themselves to their own ministry (see Acts 6:1-7). Churches should provide enough financial support for their ministers so that they can fully devote themselves to the work of the ministry.

In other words, ministers and members should labor together in the work of the Lord.

11
What to Do
Before It Ends

2 Timothy 3

The emphasis in this chapter is on *knowledge* and *responsibility*. Paul informed Timothy about the character of the last days, and then Paul instructed Timothy how to respond. Action must be based on knowledge. Too many Christians are like the pilot who informed his passengers, "We are lost, but we are making very good time."

"These last days" began with the ministry of Jesus Christ (Heb. 1:1-2) and will continue until He returns. They are called the "last days" because in them God is completing His purposes for His people. Because our Lord has delayed His return, some people scoff at the promise of His coming (2 Peter 3:3ff); but He will come as He promised.

Within this period of "last days" there will be "times" (seasons) of different kinds; but as the "times" draw to a close, they will become perilous. This word means "dangerous, hard to deal with, savage." This is the same Greek word that is used to describe the two violent demoniacs of Gadara (Matt. 8:28). This suggests that the violence of the last times will be energized by demons (1 Tim. 4:1).

There is no doubt that these characteristics started to appear in Paul's day, and now they have increased in intensity. It is not simply that we have more people in the world, or better news coverage. It appears that evil is deeper and of greater intensity, and that it is being accepted and promoted by society in a bolder way. It is not that we have small pockets of rebellion here and there. All of society seems to be in ferment and rebellion. We are indeed in "terrible times" (2 Tim. 3:1, NIV).

Paul gave Timothy three instructions to obey in order that his ministry might be effective during perilous times:

1. Turn away from the false (2 Tim. 3:1-9)

"From such turn away!" (3:5b) A faithful believer should have nothing to do with the people Paul described in this section. It is important to note that these people operate *under the guise of religion:* "having a form of godliness, but denying the power thereof" (3:5). They are "religious" but rebellious! Paul discussed three facts about these people:

A. THEIR CHARACTERISTICS (2 TIM. 3:2-5). At least 18 different characteristics are listed here, and Paul probably could have listed more. There is an emphasis on *love:* "lovers of their own selves," lovers of money ("covetous"), "lovers of pleasures more than lovers of God." The heart of every problem is a problem in the heart. God commands us to love Him supremely, and our neighbors as ourselves (Matt. 22:34-40); but if we love ourselves supremely, we will not love God *or* our neighbors.

In this universe there is God, and there are "people"

and "things." We should worship God, love people, and use things. But if we start worshiping ourselves, we will ignore God and start loving things and using people. This is the formula for a miserable life; yet it characterizes many people today. The worldwide craving for *things* is just one evidence that people's hearts have turned away from God.

Of course, if someone loves and worships himself, the result will be *pride*. "Ye shall be as gods" was Satan's offer to Eve (Gen. 3:5), and the result was that people "changed the truth of God into a lie, and worshiped and served the creature more than [rather than] the Creator" (Rom. 1:25). Man became his own God! The creature is now the creator! "Boasters, proud [arrogant], blasphemers [given to contemptuous and bitter words] " (2 Tim. 3:2).

"Disobedient to parents" suggests that this apostasy reaches into the family. Children are "unthankful" and do not appreciate what their parents have done for them. They are "unholy" in their attitude toward their parents. "Honor thy father and thy mother" is no longer taught or respected.

The phrase "without natural affection" is the translation of one word that describes "family love." The family is under attack these days, and as goes its families, so goes the nation.

In place of the natural love that God has put into men and women and families, today we have a good deal of *un*natural love which God has condemned (see Rom. 1:18-27; 1 Cor. 6:9-10). It is confusion, and God will judge it (Rom. 1:28-32).

Not only in homes, but out in society and the business world, the characteristics of these perilous times may be seen. "Trucebreakers" (2 Tim. 3:3) describes people who will not try to agree. They are unyielding and irreconcilable and must have their own way.

In order to defend their position, they become "slanderers" ["false accusers," kjv] and try to tear down the reputations of others. Unfortunately, some of this activity goes on even among professed Christians. "Christian leaders" accuse one another in the pages of their publications.

"Incontinent" means "without self-control." The motto of society today is, "Do your own thing and enjoy it!" Sad to say, some of the children born to these people do not always enjoy it, because they are deformed or handicapped as the result of drugs, alcohol, or venereal diseases.

This lack of self-control reveals itself in a number of ways. "Fierce" means "untamed, brutal." When these people cannot have their way, they become like savage beasts. Instead of honoring what is good, they despise what is good and honor what is evil. In society today, the standards of right and wrong have been twisted, if not destroyed. "Woe unto them that call evil good and good evil," cried Isaiah the prophet (Isa. 5:20).

"Traitors" (2 Tim. 3:4) describes people who betray others and cannot be trusted. Neither friendship nor partnership makes any difference to them; they lie and break their promises whenever doing so helps them get their own way.

"Heady" means "reckless, rash, acting without careful thought." Paul did not condemn honest adventure, but foolish endeavor.

"High-minded" does not describe a person with lofty thoughts. Rather, it means a person who is "puffed up" with his own importance. "Conceited" is a good synonym.

"Lovers of pleasures more than lovers of God" does not suggest that we must choose between pleasure and

God; for when we live for God, we enjoy the greatest
pleasures (Ps. 16:11). The choice is between *loving*
pleasure or loving God. If we love God, we will also
enjoy fullness of life here and forever; but the pleasures of sin last only for a brief time (Heb. 11:25). No
one can deny that we live in a pleasure-mad world; but
these pleasures too often are just shallow entertainment and escape; they are not enrichment and true
enjoyment.

Paul stated that these people he has just described
would consider themselves religious! "Having a form
of godliness" (2 Tim. 3:5) suggests an outward appearance of religion, not true Christian faith; for they have
never experienced the power of God in their lives.
Form without force. Religion without reality.

B. THEIR CONVERTS (2 TIM. 3:6-7). The fact that Paul
described "silly ['weak-willed,' NIV] women" does not
suggest that all women are like this, or that men are not
vulnerable to the wiles of false teachers. In Paul's day,
women were especially susceptible to this kind of experience since they had a low status in society.
Whether they are men or women, people who fall for
this false religious system have the same characteristics.

They are *burdened with guilt* and looking for some
escape from bondage and fear. They find themselves
unable to control their various desires ("divers lusts,"
KJV). The emphasis here may be on sexual problems.
Finally, they are always searching for truth, trying this
approach and that; yet they are never able to be satisfied. This kind of person is fair bait for the cultists and
the religious racketeers.

These false religious leaders take advantage of the
problems people have, and promise them quick and
easy solutions. They "worm their way in" and soon

control people's lives. It is not long before these leaders grab their followers' loyalty, money, and service. And their "converts" are worse off than they were before. They still have their problems, but they have been duped into thinking that all is well.

And, remember: All of this underhanded activity is done in the name of religion! No wonder Paul told Timothy, "From such, turn away!"

C. THEIR RELIGIOUS LEADERS (2 TIM. 3:8-9). Read Exodus 7—9 for the record of the contest between Moses and the Egyptian magicians. Tradition says that the magicians were Jannes and Jambres, two men mentioned by Paul (2 Tim. 3:8). These men opposed Moses *by imitating what he did*. When Aaron's rod turned into a serpent, the magicians cast down their rods and they turned into serpents. Moses turned the water into blood, and the magicians followed with the same miracle. When Moses brought up all the frogs, the magicians duplicated the miracle. But when it came to the miracle of the lice, the magicians could not imitate it (Ex. 8:16-19).

Satan is an imitator; what God does, Satan counterfeits. The religious leaders in the last days will have a counterfeit faith, and their purpose is to promote a lie and resist the truth of God's Word. They deny the authority of the Bible and substitute human wisdom and philosophy. In their attempt to be "modern," they deny the reality of sin and people's need for salvation. "Reprobate" is the word Paul used to describe them. This means "tested and found counterfeit."

Jannes and Jambres were finally exposed and made fools of by the judgments of God. This will also happen to the leaders of false religions in the last days. When God's judgments fall, the true character of these counterfeits will be revealed to everyone.

2. Follow those who are true (2 Tim. 3:10-12)

Paul turned from the false leaders to remind Timothy that he (Paul) had been a faithful servant of God. It is important in these difficult days that we follow the right spiritual leaders. What are their characteristics?

A. THEIR LIVES ARE OPEN FOR ALL TO SEE (2 TIM. 3:10). Paul had nothing to hide. Like his Master, he could say, "In secret have I said nothing" (John 18:20). "My manner of life from my youth . . . know all the Jews," Paul had told Agrippa (Acts 26:4). Timothy had lived and labored with Paul and knew the man well. Paul had not hidden behind extravagant claims or religious propaganda.

B. THEY TEACH TRUE DOCTRINE (2 TIM. 3:10). "My doctrine" in Paul's case meant the true faith, the Gospel of Jesus Christ. No matter how appealing a preacher may be, if he does not preach the truth of God's Word, he does not deserve our support. On radio and TV today, we have a great deal of "pseudo-Christianity" which is a mixture of psychology, success motivation, and personality cults, with a little bit of Bible thrown in to make it look religious. Beware!

C. THEY PRACTICE WHAT THEY PREACH (2 TIM. 3:10). Paul's "manner of life" backed up his messages. He did not preach sacrifice and live in luxury. He gave to others far more than he received from them. He stood up for the truth even when it meant losing friends and, in the end, losing his life. Paul was a servant, not a celebrity.

D. THEIR PURPOSE IS TO GLORIFY GOD (2 TIM. 3:10). There was never a question about Paul's "purpose" in ministry: He wanted to do God's will and finish the work God gave him to do (Acts 20:24; Phil. 1:21). Paul was a man of "faith" who trusted God to meet his needs. He was a man of "long-suffering" who bore up under people's attacks. He was a man of *love* ("charity") who willingly gave himself to serve others.

The word "patience" at the end of 2 Timothy 3:10 means "endurance, the ability to stick with it when the going gets tough."

E. THEY ARE WILLING TO SUFFER (2 TIM. 3:11-12). Paul did not ask others to suffer for him; *he suffered for others*. The fact that he was persecuted from city to city was proof that he was living a godly life. Some people today have the idea that godliness means *escaping* persecution, when just the opposite is true.

I wonder how Paul would match up with today's concept of a Christian leader. He would probably fail miserably. If he applied for service with a modern mission board, would he be accepted? He had a prison record; he had a physical affliction; he stirred up problems in just about every place he visited. He was poor, and he did not cater to the rich. Yet God used him, and we are being blessed today because Paul was faithful.

3. Continue in God's Word
(2 Tim. 3:13-17)

The only way to defeat Satan's lies is with God's truth. "Thus saith the Lord!" is the final answer to every question. Evil men and deceivers are going to get worse and worse. They will deceive more and more. Why? Because they are being deceived by Satan! In these last days, there will be more deception and imitation; and the only way a believer will be able to tell the true from the false is by knowing the Word of God.

Timothy had been taught the Word of God from a child. Some people are prone to say, "Well, I needed the Bible when I was younger; but I can do without it now that I'm older." How wrong they are! Adults need the guidance of the Word far more than children do, because adults face more temptations and make more decisions. Timothy's grandmother and mother had faithfully taught him the Old Testament Scriptures (the word "whom" in v. 14 is plural, referring to these women; see 1:5). Timothy was to continue in what he had been taught. We never outgrow the Word of God.

This is a good place to admonish Christian parents to teach their children the Bible. In our home, my wife and I used Kenneth Taylor's *Bible Stories with Pictures for Little Eyes;* in fact, we wore out two copies! What a joy it was to see our older children who had learned to read share the stories with the younger ones, and help them answer the questions. Little by little, the children graduated to older Bible storybooks and then to Bibles of their own. We were fortunate that our Sunday School included a Bible memory program. As soon as your child is born, surround him with the Word of God and prayer. You will not have this opportunity after he grows up.

In this paragraph, Paul made some important statements about the Scriptures:

A. THEY ARE THE HOLY SCRIPTURES (2 TIM. 3:15). "The sacred letters" is a literal translation. The suggestion is that young Timothy learned his Hebrew alphabet by spelling his way through the Old Testament Scriptures. The word for "holy" means "consecrated for sacred use." The Bible is different from every other book—even books about the Bible—because it has been set apart by God for special sacred uses. We must treat the Bible as the special book it is.

The way we treat the Bible shows others how much or how little we respect it. While I don't want to become a crank in this matter, I must confess that I hate to see a Bible on the floor. When we are carrying a Bible and other books, the Bible should be on the top. There is a difference between properly marking a Bible as we study, and defacing it by careless marking. I have seen people put a cup of coffee on a Bible! Paul gives us the right attitude toward the Word of God (1 Thes. 2:13).

B. THE SCRIPTURES LEAD US TO SALVATION (2 TIM. 3:15). We are not saved by believing the Bible (see John 5:39), but by trusting the Christ who is revealed in the Bible. Satan knows the Bible but he is not saved. Timothy was raised on the Holy Scriptures in a godly home. Yet it was not until Paul led him to Christ that he was saved.

What is the relationship of the Bible to salvation? To begin with, the Bible reveals our need for salvation. It is a mirror that shows us how filthy we are in God's sight. The Bible explains that every lost sinner is condemned *now* (John 3:18-21) and needs a Saviour *now*. It also makes it clear that a lost sinner cannot save himself.

But the Bible also reveals God's wonderful plan of salvation: Christ died for our sins! If we trust Him, He will save us (John 3:16-18). The Bible also helps give us the assurance of our salvation (see 1 John 5:9-13). Then the Bible becomes our spiritual food to nourish us that we might grow in grace and serve Christ. It is our sword for fighting Satan and overcoming temptation.

C. THE SCRIPTURES ARE TRUE AND DEPENDABLE (2 TIM. 3:16A). "All Scripture is God-breathed" (NIV). The doctrine of the inspiration of Scripture is vitally important, and a doctrine that Satan has attacked from the beginning ("Yea, hath God said?" Gen. 3:1). It is inconceivable that God would give His people a book they could not trust. He is the God of truth (Deut. 32:4); Jesus is "the truth" (John 14:6); and the "Spirit is truth" (1 John 5:6). Jesus said of the Scriptures, "Thy Word is truth" (John 17:17).

The Holy Spirit of God used men of God to write the Word of God (2 Peter 1:20-21). The Spirit did not erase the natural characteristics of the writers. In fact, God in His providence prepared the writers for the task of writing the Scriptures. Each writer has his own distinctive style and vocabulary. Each book of the Bible grew out of a special set of circumstances. In His preparation of men, in His guiding of history, and in His working through the Spirit, God brought about the miracle of the Scriptures.

We must not think of "inspiration" the way the world thinks when it says, "Shakespeare was certainly an inspired writer." What we mean by biblical *inspiration* is that supernatural influence of the Holy Spirit on the Bible's writers which guaranteed that what they wrote was accurate and trustworthy. *Revelation* means the communicating of truth to man by God; *inspiration* has to do with the *recording* of this communication in a way that is dependable.

Whatever the Bible says about itself, man, God, life, death, history, science, and every other subject is true. This does not mean that every statement in the Bible is true, because the Bible records the lies of men and of Satan. *But the record is true.*

D. THE SCRIPTURES ARE PROFITABLE (2 TIM. 3:16B). They are profitable for *doctrine* (what is right), for *reproof* (what is not right), for *correction* (how to get right), and for *instruction in righteousness* (how to stay right). A Christian who studies the Bible and applies what he learns will grow in holiness and avoid many pitfalls in this world.

E. The Scriptures equip us for service (2 Tim. 3:17). Earlier Paul had called Timothy a "man of God" (1 Tim. 6:11); but here Paul states that *any* Christian can become a person "of God." How? By studying the Word of God, obeying it, and letting it control his life. It is worth noting that all of the "men of God" named in Scripture—including Moses, Samuel, Elijah, Elisha, David, and Timothy—were men who were devoted to God's Word.

Two words in this verse are especially important: "perfect" and "furnished." The word translated "perfect" means "complete, in fit shape, in fit condition." It does not begin to suggest sinless perfection. Rather, it implies being fitted for use.

"Furnished" has a similar meaning: "equipped for service." In other words, the Word of God furnishes and equips a believer so that he can live a life that pleases God and do the work God wants him to do. The better we know the Word, the better we are able to live and work for God.

The purpose of Bible study is *not* just to understand doctrines, or to be able to defend the faith, as important as these things are. The ultimate purpose is the equipping of the believers who read it. It is the Word of God that equips God's people to do the work of God.

The times are not going to get better, but we Christians can become better people, even in bad times. We must separate ourselves from that which is false, devote ourselves to that which is true, and continue in our study of the Word of God. Then God can equip us for ministry in these difficult days, and we will have the joy of seeing others come to a knowledge of the truth.

12
Last Words

2 Timothy 4

A great person's last words are significant. They are a window that helps us to look into his heart, or a measure that helps us evaluate his life. In this chapter, we have Paul's last words to Timothy and to the church.

It is interesting that Paul expressed no regrets as he came to the end. He even forgave those who made his situation difficult (4:16). More than 17 persons are referred to in this chapter, which shows that Paul was a friend-maker as well as a soul-winner. Though his own days were numbered, Paul thought of others.

The apostle gave three final admonitions to Timothy, and he backed each of them up with a reason.

1. Preach the Word! (2 Tim. 4:1-4)

"I charge thee" should read "I solemnly witness." This was a serious moment and Paul wanted Timothy to sense the importance of it. It was serious, not only because Paul was facing death, but even more because both Paul and Timothy would be judged one day when Jesus Christ appeared. It would do us all good to occasionally reflect on the fact that one day we will face God and our works will be judged.

For one thing, this realization would encourage us to do our work carefully and faithfully. It would also deliver us from the fear of man; for, after all, our final Judge is God. Finally, the realization that God will one day judge our works encourages us to keep going even when we face difficulties. We are serving Him, not ourselves.

"Preach the Word!" is the main responsibility that Paul shared in this section. Everything else he said is related to this. The word "preach" means "to preach like a herald." In Paul's day, a ruler had a special herald who made announcements to the people. He was commissioned by the ruler to make his announcements in a loud, clear voice so everyone could hear. He was not an ambassador with the privilege of negotiating; he was a messenger with a proclamation to be heard and heeded. Not to heed the ruler's messenger was serious; to abuse the messenger was even worse.

Timothy was to herald God's Word with the authority of heaven behind him. The Word of God is what both sinners and saints need. It is a pity that many churches have substituted other things for the preaching of the Word, things that may be good in their place, but that are bad when they replace the proclamation of the Word. In my own pastoral ministry, I have seen what the preaching of the Word can do in churches and in individual lives; and I affirm that *nothing can take its place*.

Timothy should be diligent and alert to use every opportunity to preach the Word, when it is favorable and even when it is not favorable. *It is easy to make excuses when we ought to be making opportunities.* Paul himself always found an opportunity to share the

Word, whether it was in the temple courts, on a stormy sea, or even in prison. "He that observeth the wind shall not sow; and he that regardeth the clouds shall not reap" (Ecc. 11:4). Stop making excuses and get to work!

Preaching must be marked by three elements: conviction, warning, and appeal ("reprove, rebuke, exhort"). To quote an old rule of preachers, "He should afflict the comfortable and comfort the afflicted." If there is conviction but no remedy, we add to people's burdens. And if we encourage those who ought to be rebuked, we are assisting them to sin. Biblical preaching must be balanced.

God's speaker must be patient as he preaches the Word. He will not always see immediate results. He must be patient with those who oppose his preaching. Above all else, *he must preach doctrine*. He must not simply tell Bible stories, relate interesting illustrations, or read a verse and then forget it. *True preaching is the explanation and application of Bible doctrine. Anything else is just religious speechmaking.*

Paul gave the responsibility—"preach the Word" (4:2)—and he also gave the reason (4:3-4). The time would come (and it has been here for a long time!) when most people would not want the "healthy doctrine" of the Word of God. They would have carnal desires for religious novelties. Because of their "itching ears" they would accumulate teachers who would satisfy their cravings for things that disagree with God's truths. The fact that a preacher has a large congregation is not always a sign that he is preaching the truth. In fact, it may be evidence that he is tickling people's "itching ears" and giving them what they *want* to hear instead of what they *need* to hear.

It is but a short step from "itching ears" to turning

one's ears away from the truth. Once people have rejected the truth, they turn to fables (myths). It is not likely that man-made fables will convict them of sin or make them want to repent! The result is a congregation of comfortable professing Christians, listening to a comfortable religious talk that contains no Bible doctrine. These people become the prey of every false cult, because their lives lack a foundation in the Word of God. It is a recognized fact that most cultists were formerly members of churches.

Note the emphasis on Scripture: "Preach the Word . . . with . . . doctrine. . . . they will not endure sound doctrine . . . they shall turn away their ears from the truth" (4:2-4). This emphasis on sound (healthy) doctrine runs through all three of Paul's Pastoral Epistles, and this emphasis is surely needed today.

2. Fulfill your ministry (2 Tim. 4:5-8)

"Make full proof of thy ministry" means "fulfill whatever God wants you to do." Timothy's ministry would not be exactly like Paul's, but it would be important to the cause of Christ. No God-directed ministry is small or unimportant. In this final chapter, Paul named some co-laborers about whom we know nothing; yet they too had a ministry to fulfill.

A young preacher once complained to Charles Spurgeon, the famous Baptist preacher, that he did not have as big a church as he deserved.

"How many do you preach to?" Spurgeon asked.

"Oh, about 100," the man replied.

Solemnly Spurgeon said, "That will be enough to give account for on the day of judgment."

We do not measure the fulfillment of a ministry only on the basis of statistics, or on what people see. We realize that faithfulness is important and that God sees the heart. This was why Timothy had to be "sober in all things" (4:5, NASB) and carry on his ministry with seriousness of purpose. (We have met this word "sober" many times in these letters.)

Timothy was not only a preacher; he was also a soldier (2:3-4) who would have to "endure afflictions" (4:5). He had seen Paul go through sufferings on more than one occasion (3:10-12; 2 Cor. 6:1-10). Most of Timothy's sufferings would come from the "religious crowd" that did not want to hear the truth. It was the "religious crowd" that crucified Christ and that persecuted Paul and had him arrested.

"Do the work of an evangelist" (2 Tim. 4:5) would remind Timothy that all of his ministry must have soul-winning at its heart. This does not mean that every sermon should be a "sawdust trail, hell-fire-and-brimstone" message, because the saints need feeding as well. But it does mean that a preacher, no matter what he is preaching, should keep the lost souls in mind. This burden for the lost should characterize a pastor's private ministry as well. (See Acts 20:17-21 for a description of a balanced ministry.)

God has given special men to the church as evangelists (Acts 21:8; Eph. 4:11); but this does not absolve a pastor from his soul-winning responsibility. Not every preacher has the same gifts, but every preacher can share the same burden and proclaim the same saving message. A friend of mine went to hear a famous preacher, and I asked him how the message was. He replied, "There wasn't enough Gospel in it to save a flea!"

Paul gave the reason behind the responsibility (2 Tim. 4:6-8): He was about to move off the scene and Timothy would have to take his place. In this beautiful paragraph of personal testimony, you find Paul looking in three different directions:

He looked around (4:6) and realized that his time was short. He was on trial in Rome and had been through the first hearing (4:17). But Paul knew that the end was near. However, he did not tremble at the prospect of death! The two words "offered" and "departure" (4:6) tell us of his faith and confidence. "Offered" means "poured out on the altar as a drink-offering." He used the same picture in Philippians 2:7-8. In effect Paul was saying, "Caesar is not going to kill me. I am going to give my life as a sacrifice to Jesus Christ. I have been a living sacrifice, serving Him, since the day I was saved. Now I will complete that sacrifice by laying down my life for Him."

The word "departure" (2 Tim. 4:6) is a beautiful word that has many meanings. It means "to hoist anchor and set sail." Paul looked on death as a release from the world, an opportunity to "set sail" into eternity. The word also means "to take down a tent." This parallels 2 Corinthians 5:1-8, where Paul compared the death of believers to the taking down of a tent (tabernacle), in order to receive a permanent glorified body ("house not made with hands"—a glorified body, not a "mansion" in heaven).

"Departure" also has the meaning of "loosing a prisoner." Paul was facing release, not execution! "The unyoking of an ox" is another meaning of this word. Paul had been in hard service for many years. Now his Master would unyoke him and promote him to higher service.

Paul looked back (2 Tim. 4:7) and summed up his life and ministry. Two of the images here are athletic: like a determined wrestler or boxer, he had fought a good fight; and, like a runner, he had finished his lifelong race victoriously. He had kept the rules and was deserving of a prize (see Phil. 3:13-14; Acts 20:24). The third image is that of a steward who had faithfully guarded his boss' deposit: "I have kept the faith" (2 Tim. 4:7). Paul used this image often in his pastoral letters.

It is heartening to be able to look back and have no regrets. Paul was not always popular, nor was he usually comfortable; but he remained faithful. That is what really counted.

Finally, *Paul looked ahead* (4:8). A Greek or Roman athlete who was a winner was rewarded by the crowds, and usually got a laurel wreath or a garland of oak leaves. The word for "crown" is *stephanos*—the victor's crown; we get our name Stephen from this word. (The kingly crown is *diadema*, from which we get diadem.) However, Paul would not be given a fading crown of leaves; his would be a crown of righteousness that would never fade.

Jesus Christ is the "righteous Judge" who always judges correctly. Paul's judges in Rome were not righteous. If they were, they would have released him. How many times Paul had been tried in one court after another, yet now he faced his last Judge—his Lord and Saviour Jesus Christ. When you are ready to face the Lord, you need not fear the judgment of men.

The crown of righteousness is God's reward for a faithful and righteous life; and our incentive for faithfulness and holiness is the promise of the Lord's appearing. Because Paul loved His appearing and looked for it, he lived righteously and served faithfully. This is why Paul used the return of Jesus Christ as a basis for his admonitions in this chapter (see 4:1).

We are not called to be apostles; yet we can win the same crown that Paul won. If we love Christ's appearing, live in obedience to His will, and do the work He has called us to do, we will be crowned.

3. Be diligent and faithful (2 Tim. 4:9-22)

"Hurry and get here!" is the meaning of the admonition (4:9). Tychicus would take Timothy's place in Ephesus (4:12). As Timothy hurried to Rome, he could stop in Troas and get the cloak, books, and parchments (4:13). Paul probably left them there in his haste to depart. It is touching to see that, in his closing days on earth, Paul wanted his dear "son in the faith" at his side. But he was also practical: he needed his cloak for warmth, and he wanted his books for study. The "books" would be papyrus scrolls, perhaps of the Old Testament Scriptures; and the "parchments" would be books made from the skins of animals. We do not know what these "parchments" were, but we are not surprised that a scholar such as Paul wanted material for study and writing.

Before he ended the letter, Paul urged Timothy to "come before winter" (4:21). Why? All the ships would be in port during the winter since it would be too dangerous for sailing. If Timothy waited too long, he would miss his opportunity to travel to Paul; and then it would be too late.

Why should Timothy be diligent and faithful? Look at verse 10, which gives part of the answer: Some in Paul's circle were not faithful, and Paul could not depend on them. Demas is named only three times in the New Testament; yet these three citations tell a sad story of failure. Paul listed Demas along with Mark and Luke as one of his "fellow laborers" (Phile. 24). Then he is simply called "Demas" (Col. 4:14). Here (2 Tim. 4:10), it is, "Demas hath forsaken me."

Paul gave the reason: Demas "loved this present

world." He had, as a believer, "tasted . . . the powers of the world to come" (Heb. 6:5); but he preferred "this present evil world" (Gal. 1:4). In his *Pilgrim's Progress*, John Bunyan pictured Demas as the keeper of a silver mine at the Hill Lucre. Perhaps it was the love of money that enticed Demas back into the world. It must have broken Paul's heart to see Demas fail so shamefully; yet it can happen to any believer. Perhaps this explains why Paul had so much to say about riches in his pastoral letters.

Another reason why Paul wanted Timothy in Rome was because his next hearing was coming up and only Luke was with him. The believers in Rome and Ephesus who could have stood with Paul had failed him (2 Tim. 4:16); but Paul knew that Timothy would not fail him. Of course, the Lord had not failed Paul either! (4:17) The Lord had promised to stay with Paul, and He had kept His promise.

When Paul had been discouraged in Corinth, the Lord came to him and encouraged him (Acts 18:9-11). After he had been arrested in Jerusalem, Paul again was visited by the Lord and encouraged (Acts 23:11). During that terrible storm, when Paul was on board ship, the Lord had again given him strength and courage (Acts 27:22ff). Now, in that horrible Roman prison, Paul again experienced the strengthening presence of the Lord, who had promised, "I will never leave thee, nor forsake thee" (Heb. 13:5).

But note that Paul's concern was not for his own safety or comfort. It was the preaching of the Word that Gentiles might be saved. It was Paul's special calling to minister to the Gentiles (see Eph. 3); and he was not ashamed of the Gospel, even in the great city of Rome (Rom. 1:16).

What a man! His friends forsake him, and he prays

that God will forgive them. His enemies try him, and he looks for opportunities to tell them how to be saved! What a difference it makes when the Holy Spirit controls your life.

"I was delivered out of the mouth of the lion" (2 Tim. 4:17). Who or what is this "lion"? It cannot mean a literal lion, because Paul was a Roman citizen and, if convicted, he could not be thrown to the lions. Instead he would be executed by being beheaded. Was "the lion" the Emperor Nero? Probably not. If he had been delivered from Nero, then this meant he was acquitted; yet, he had only had a preliminary first hearing. The lion is a symbol of Satan (1 Peter 5:8). Perhaps Paul was referring to some scheme of the devil to defeat him and hinder the work of the Gospel. To be "saved from the lion's mouth" was a proverbial saying which meant "to be delivered from great danger" (Ps. 22:21).

But, for a Christian, there are even more dangerous things than suffering and death. Sin, for example. This is what Paul had in mind (2 Tim. 4:18). He was confident that the Lord would deliver him from "every evil work" and take him to the heavenly kingdom. Paul's greatest fear was not of death; it was that he might deny his Lord or do something else that would disgrace God's name. Paul was certain that the time had come for his permanent departure (4:6). He wanted to end his life-race well and be free from any disobedience.

It is heartening to see how many persons are named in the closing part of this last letter Paul wrote. I believe that there are at least 100 different men and women named in Acts and Paul's letters, as a part of his circle of friends and fellow laborers. Paul could not do the job by himself. It is a great man who enlists others to help get the job done, and who lets them share in the greatness of the work.

Luke (4:11) is the "beloved physician" who traveled with Paul (Col. 4:14). He is author of the Gospel of Luke and the Book of Acts. (Notice the "we" sections in Acts, the eyewitness reports of Dr. Luke.) Paul probably dictated this letter (2 Tim.) to Luke. Being a doctor, Luke must have appreciated Paul's reference to "gangrene" (2:17, NIV).

Crescens (4:10) was sent by Paul to Galatia. We know nothing about him, nor do we need to know. He was another faithful laborer who assisted Paul in an hour of great need.

Titus (4:10) was Paul's close associate and, along with Timothy, a trusted "troubleshooter." Paul had left Titus in Crete to straighten out the problems in the churches there (Titus 1:5). As we studied Paul's letter to Titus, we got better acquainted with this choice servant of God. Titus had met Paul at Nicopolis during that period between Paul's arrests (Titus 3:12). Now Paul had summoned him to Rome and sent him to Dalmatia (our modern Yugoslavia).

Mark (2 Tim. 4:11) was a cousin of Barnabas, Paul's first partner in missionary service (Acts 13:1-3). His mother was a noted Christian in Jerusalem (Acts 12:5, 12). Unfortunately, John Mark failed on that first missionary journey (Acts 13:5, 13). Paul refused to take Mark on the second trip, and this led to a falling out between Paul and Barnabas (Acts 15:36-41). However, Paul now admitted that John Mark was a valuable worker; and he wanted Mark with him in Rome. How good it is to know that one failure in Christian service need not make one's whole life a failure.

Tychicus (2 Tim. 4:12) was a believer from the province of Asia (Acts 20:4) who willingly accompanied Paul and probably ministered as a personal servant to the apostle. He was with Paul during his first imprisonment (Col. 4:7-8; Eph. 6:21-22). Paul sent Tychicus to Crete to relieve Titus (Titus 3:12). Now he was sending him to Ephesus to relieve Timothy. What a blessing it is to have people who can replace others! A relief pitcher may not get all the glory, but he may help win the game!

Carpus (2 Tim. 4:13) lived at Troas and gave Paul hospitality when he needed it. Paul must have departed in a hurry (was he being sought for arrest?) because he left his cloak and books behind. However, Carpus was a faithful brother; he would guard them until somebody picked them up to take to Paul. Even such so-called menial tasks are ministries for the Lord.

Is *"Alexander the coppersmith"* (4:14) the same Alexander mentioned in 1 Timothy 1:20? Nobody knows, and there is no value in conjecturing. The name was common, but it is possible that this heretic went to Rome to make things difficult for Paul. Satan has his workers, too. By the way, Paul's words, "The Lord reward him according to his works" (2 Tim. 4:14) are not a prayer of judgment; for this would be contrary to Jesus' teaching (Matt. 5:43-48). "The Lord *will* reward him" is a better translation.

Prisca [or Priscilla] *and Aquila* (2 Tim. 4:19) were a husband and wife team that assisted Paul in many ways (see Acts 18:1-3, 24-28; Rom. 16:3-4; 1 Cor. 16:19). Now they were in Ephesus helping Timothy with his ministry. It is wonderful when God's people do their work regardless of who their leader is.

Onesiphorus (2 Tim. 4:19) and his household we have met in chapter 1.

Erastus (4:20) might be the treasurer of Corinth (Rom. 16:23); and he might be the same man who ministered with Timothy in Macedonia (Acts 19:22).

Trophimus (2 Tim. 4:20) from Ephesus, was a friend of Tychicus (Acts 20:4), and the man whose presence with Paul helped to incite that riot in Jerusalem (Acts 21:28-29). He had been serving at Miletus, but now he was ill. Why did Paul not heal him? Apparently not every sick person is supposed to be miraculously healed.

The other people mentioned (2 Tim. 4:21) are unknown to us, but certainly not to the Lord.

"Grace be with you" (4:22) was Paul's personal farewell, used at the end of his letters as a "trademark" that the letter was not a forgery.

The Bible does not record the final days of Paul. Tradition tells us that he was found guilty and sentenced to die. He was probably taken outside the city and beheaded.

But Timothy and the other devoted believers carried on the work! As John Wesley used to say, "God buries His workmen, but His work goes on." You and I must be faithful so that (if the Lord does not return soon) future generations may hear the Gospel and have the opportunity to be saved.

Be faithful—it's always too soon to quit!